H
WONDROUS
CROSS

The story of our redemption

BRIAN D. JONES

Pacific Press® Publishing Association
Nampa, Idaho
Oshawa, Ontario, Canada
www.pacificpress.com

Designed by Dennis Ferree
Cover illustration by Justinen Creative Group

Copyright © 2004 by
Pacific Press® Publishing Association
Printed in United States of America

Except where otherwise noted, all Scripture quotations
are from the King James Version.

Additional copies of this book are available by calling toll free
1-800-765-6955 or by visiting
<http://www.adventistbookcenter.com>.

ISBN: 0-8163-2033-0

04 05 06 07 08 • 5 4 3 2 1

Contents

Foreword

Until I was twenty-three, Christ and Calvary meant nothing to me. Since childhood I had thought of Christianity as synonymous with fraud and deception. I felt arrogant pity for those who were naive enough to be Christians, people who clung to defunct creeds and gloomy symbols—especially the Cross. But my soul was acutely hungry for spiritual meaning.

In quest of truth, I explored all the major world religions—from animism to Zen—except for Christianity. Eventually I formed my own eclectic mélange of beliefs, tailored with precision to the warped contours of my ego. My religion was basically a hybrid of Hinduism, hallucinogens, jazz, Zen, and loosely strung social ideals that called for benevolence to people like me. In short, I was self-centered and confused.

But in the midst of these clouded views of life, I sensed a deep need for justification. Not justification in the biblical sense, but rather a perversion of it. For example, I justified my drinking and drugging on the grounds that doing so enabled me to play jazz and write poetry with more freedom. I justified my earthly sojourn by voluntarily picking up garbage on the roadside and taking it to the county dump. I was engaging in the age-old exercise of trying to establish my own righteousness by the performance of "meritorious" deeds, which in my case were of slender virtue at best. Peace eluded me, and so did purity of mind and nobility of conduct.

Yet in my own circuitous, shambling way I was seeking for truth that would bring me into harmony with the Over-Soul, as Emerson called it, the Creative Intelligence of the universe. Often disquieted by a sense of final accountability, I wondered what excuses I could offer for dissipating my energies in selfish, unproductive living. Who on earth was I benefiting by my existence? Yet, though I was afraid to go on, I was powerless to make a change.

By degrees I saw that drunkenness, sensuality, and detachment from society could hardly foster spiritual development. I read many books on mysticism, but they offered such a jumble of divergent possibilities that I began to feel like I was in the midst of a parching desert without chart or compass, surrounded with shimmering mirages and no oasis anywhere.

While vastly dissimilar in some respects, most of the false systems of religion held one proposition in common. They said that every person is fundamentally divine; people need only find the spiritual discipline that enables them to discover and develop their godlike essence. This lie entertained me for several years. However, the longer I lived, the more confused and degenerate I became, buffeted by the erratic winds of passion, craving, and fear. Somehow the suggestion that my cohorts in debauchery and I were innately divine strained my credulity. In fact, we all seemed like fools—I especially, because I found no answers to my persistent questions.

Then, unexpectedly, I began meeting Christians. If I gave them a chance to testify of their beliefs, they all mentioned Jesus as the One who was crucified for their sins and who was now the Lord and Savior of their lives. This declaration of faith seemed to issue from a genuine experience that gave them great joy. I was both attracted and repelled by such testimonies. At times, under the compelling influence of these witnesses, I was almost persuaded to be a Christian. I knew that I needed spiritual renovation. And it was clear to me by now that no drug, no meditation technique, no deeds of valor or beneficence would provide that renovation because none of them could dispel my inner darkness and depravity, my coldness, my sour selfishness and incapacity to love freely.

However, the idea of becoming a Christian in order to be a new person was repugnant to my pride. I wanted to find something *I could do* to bring about the necessary changes in my life. Perhaps, I hoped, some philosophy sanitized of all superstition would put me on the pathway of upright living. Or maybe I needed to embrace some artistic discipline to put me in tune with cosmic reality.

Often I contemplated the matter of Jesus' promises and claims and uneasily discussed them with friends and acquaintances who had become Christian. I wondered how people could degrade themselves to worship a God who was tortured to death by some religious bigots who disagreed with His program. I thought God should be immune to that kind of treatment. And then, this idea of confessing oneself to be a helpless sinner in need of salvation—it was too humiliating. It exposed one to ridicule by the worldly wise and manipulation by religious parasites all too ready to hear confessions and take control of the conscience.

Objections to Christianity

As I resisted the conviction of my need for Jesus' salvation, objections to Christianity began to pile up mountainously high. But I had no peace, and my spiritual life assumed increasingly chaotic overtones. Amid my angry darkness, the cross of Jesus was from time to time illuminated to my mind with a strangely beckoning light. But I writhed uncomfortably in the face of the vision. I didn't want to give up alcohol, jazz, and the liberty to do as I pleased—or rather, to do what the lusts of the flesh drove me to do. Yet the Christians I knew had peace, kindness, decency, compassion, and a freedom from fear that both puzzled and attracted me. Why couldn't I get what they had without having to lower myself to their beliefs? It was agony to live; it was still greater agony to contemplate death and the day of ultimate reckoning.

Then one day, after a night of shameless debauch with drunken strangers, I started out in the early morning hours to my hut in the woods. As I trudged homeward in the grey light of dawn and sensed the futility and declining value of my life, the words welled up in my heart, "God, I must have Your truth, even if it means becoming a Christian."

At this point the Holy Spirit, knowing the peculiarities of my mind, began a rational dialogue with me. The thought came clearly to me, *If Christ is God, as Christians maintain He is, then He must have all knowledge and all power.* I could agree with this hypothesis, being convinced that God, being eternal and infinite, must by definition possess all power and all knowledge.

So, if Christ is God, He must have voluntarily committed Himself as a sacrifice for the sins of humanity, because He could not be robbed of His life unwillingly. This proposition also made sense.

And if Christ, though God, became a man to die voluntarily for your sins, doesn't it behoove you to become acquainted with such a merciful and loving God as this, and commit your life to His care and authority? I couldn't deny the logic of this position. And because the same Spirit convinced me that Christ is indeed God, I felt it would be inexcusable obstinacy to withhold myself from Him.

Not long afterward I became acquainted with Jesus' statement, " 'I, if I am lifted up from the earth, will draw all peoples to Myself.' This He said, signifying by what death He would die" (John 12:32, 33, NKJV). I also discovered the truth of the following statement:

> The Spirit is constantly seeking to draw the attention of men to the great offering that was made on the cross of Calvary, to unfold to the world the love of God, and to open to the convicted soul the precious things of the Scriptures.[1]

The cross is no longer an object of loathing to me. It has become the tree of life to my soul, the instrument of my salvation, the mainstay of my comfort, the inspiration of my service, the bulwark of my values, the monitor of my conscience, the gateway of my liberty, and, as with the repentant thief, the trysting place of my hopes. Without the cross of Jesus, life on this earth would be devoid of meaning, destitute of hope. But with the Cross, the prospects of redemption, righteousness, and renewal are overflowingly abundant and available to all. I write this book as a former rebel against the government of God, now cheerfully reporting for duty and pledging allegiance to the conquering Hero of Calvary, who has conquered my heart by the solemn power and majesty of His love displayed on the cross.

---

1. Ellen G. White, *Acts of the Apostles* (Nampa, Idaho: Pacific Press®, 1911), 52.

Introduction

Today the cross is an object of reverence. Found in churches, embossed on book covers, engraved in furniture, erected as sculpture, enshrined in paintings, worn as jewelry, exalted in sermon and song, the cross is Christianity's identifying badge. Preeminent symbol of religious faith in our world, it has revolutionized society as nothing else could, for its power is infinite and eternal. Fervently appreciated by some, it is largely misunderstood by many, being invoked at times as a bond of exemption from obedience to God and viewed as a magic charm against disasters caused by human folly. Yet the Cross shall ultimately eradicate all the errors, corruption, and misdeeds of humanity, and all the residue of Satan's mischief.

Not that the cross in itself has any power. Rather it is the One who voluntarily hung upon it that invests it with its fathomless might and majesty. Although we may contemplate the Cross with endless profit, no one can exhaustively explain it. Embodying as it does God's infinite wisdom and love, it will disclose its boundless treasures to reverent minds throughout eternity.

The great achievements of soldiers, philosophers, statesmen, and poets of previous generations gradually fade in significance, but the grandeur of Christ's cross increases with the passage of time. Yet time itself contributes nothing; it is the Cross that changes time and life into a loom on which God weaves a tapestry depicting the immortal splendor of all that Christ wrought out on Calvary for the eternal benefit of the universe.

CHAPTER

The Bane and the Antidote

It was a frustrating situation. More than that, it was desperate and dangerous. Catapulted into World War II by Japan's attack on Pearl Harbor, America could keep none of its military and naval movements secret. Axis forces had broken the Allies' military codes and could readily decipher all transmitted messages. But American actions in the Pacific could not succeed without secrecy.

As American cryptologists futilely strove to invent unbreakable codes, Philip Johnston, an American missionary to the Navajo, remembered how thoroughly mystified the Germans had been in World War I as the Choctaws conversed freely over radio to convey critical messages that helped the Allied forces to victory. Philip Johnston spoke Navajo fluently. He knew that though government teachers appointed to Americanize the Navajo had striven to eradicate their richly expressive tongue in favor of English, the freedom-loving Navajo had refused to be driven into submission. And he knew that few non-Navajo were acquainted with this difficult language.

At Philip Johnston's urging, the War Department decided to establish a corps of Navajo "code talkers" to whom would be entrusted the secure information that had to pass quickly between American fleets and squadrons during their tactical moves. These Navajo code talkers devised hundreds of military terms and memorized them, leaving no written materials that could be captured.

Throughout the war their unique language remained a mystery to Japanese cryptologists, allowing American nautical movements to take place with much less interference than before. Navajo code talkers played a vital role in every assault conducted by the U.S. Marines from 1942 to 1945, including the one on Iwo Jima. So it was that America's most effective secret military weapon during World War II was an ancient language. Ironically, the language that the United States sought to obliterate became the shield of its security and the sword of its triumph.

For many, God's Word is as incomprehensible as the encrypted Navajo of World War II's code talkers. They find prophecy as puzzling as hieroglyphics, and the basic doctrine of Scripture seems to them like twaddle (see Daniel 12:8-10; 1 Corinthians 2:12-14). However, there is a vital difference between the Navajo encryption and the Bible. The Navajo code was meant to be understood only by a small number of initiated men, but God means for all to understand His Word and to follow its guiding light (see Psalm 119:105; Proverbs 6:23).

Japanese intelligence officials labored desperately to crack the code that exposed their naval and air movements and facilitated those of their adversary. In contrast, many regard the Bible as a book of so little consequence that if they ever open it, they peruse it languidly. Others try to crack the code of advanced theological constructs in Scripture by the use of their rational powers and linguistic skills. But they miss the essential power and beauty of the Bible's message because they do not approach it as humble learners in the school of Christ. The Bible is so simple that an attentive child can understand most of it. But that which is spiritual is spiritually discerned, and the Bible is a spiritual book.

Hidden From the Wise

In Jesus are hidden all the treasures of wisdom and knowledge. He says, " 'Learn from Me, for I am gentle and lowly in heart.' " Before the conceited doctors of the law He declared, " 'I thank You, Father, Lord of heaven and earth, because You have hidden these things from the wise and prudent and have revealed them to babes.

Even so, Father, for so it seemed good in Your sight' " (Matthew 11:29, 25, 26, NKJV).

God's Word does not disclose its treasures to the casual seeker, nor to the scornful inquirer, nor to the enemies of truth who seek to decode the sacred volume only to mock its devotees. No degree of scholarship can construct a tower so tall and sturdy as to reach the heights of Heaven's wisdom. God declares, "My thoughts are not your thoughts, neither are your ways my ways. . . . For as the heavens are higher than the earth, so are my ways higher than your ways, and my thoughts than your thoughts" (Isaiah 55:8, 9). We must wait quietly before the Lord, and prayerfully ask Him to open our eyes that we might behold wondrous things out of His law and discern the glories of His gospel with unclouded vision. No matter how limited our present knowledge and powers of comprehension, if we're willing to do God's will, then we shall understand His truth (see John 7:17).

Those who study the Bible to discover God's original order and the beginning and end of evil begin their study with the right objective. If, however, in our deluded intellectuality we turn God's revelation of these basic issues into a myth or an allegory, then for us the plan of salvation becomes mystic vapor, a mere fairy tale for simpletons.

God's Word bears the protective seal of its divine Author so that the Scripture cannot be broken (see Psalm 12:6, 7; Isaiah 40:8; John 10:35). It discloses its treasures to the brokenhearted who seek wholeness on God's terms and for His honor. Taking this approach to the entire subject of Christ's cross, from its first foreshadowings to its starkly sublime accomplishment on Calvary, opens the doors of perception to the fundamental issues of life that have occupied philosophers for centuries. Our understanding of these issues fashions the direction and destiny of our lives.

How did it all begin? How did the need for Jesus' sacrifice arise? What is the reason for all the desolation and disarray that we see in our world socially and morally? These questions become particularly pressing if we start with the foundational belief that God is love. Certainly the murder, violence, warfare, crime, vice, profanity, and brutal entertainment that shape life on earth are not manifestations

11

of love but of its very opposite. So why all this twistedness that we call evil—this cruel impetus that drives people to invent stories that exalt vileness and deride decency, to sell mind-destroying drugs, to blow up buses carrying school children, to drop bombs on cities, to ram airliners into crowded office buildings?

In His Word, God declares that He created the world and that everything He made was very good. He made Adam and Eve in His own image, innate partakers of His divine goodness (see Psalm 25:8; Ecclesiastes 7:29). *Yashar*, the root word in Hebrew translated "upright," has connotations of "straight," "even," "proper," "seemly," "equitable," and "good." It's no surprise then that Scripture associates evil with crookedness, the root word for which in Hebrew is *akal*, which literally means to "wrest" or "twist" or to "pervert" (see Deuteronomy 32:5; Psalm 125:5; Proverbs 2:5).

God's original creation was entirely free from the anguish that sin has since brought into the universe. Every intelligent being knew that God is love. All served Him with boundless joy and delight. No pain or fear marred the perfect happiness of God's creatures. No shadow of egotism, impurity, violence, or vexation crossed the path of any. No doubts arose concerning the Creator's wisdom and perfect love toward all.

But God knew from the start that a hidden risk accompanied His imparting to every rational being a special gift that He could not bear to withhold—the gift of free choice. He knew that without freedom of choice, life would be a sham—an intricate marionette show in which He pulled all the strings. Such an arrangement could not bring satisfaction to God or His creatures, for they would be no more than robots with a simulated identity and a mock allegiance to their Creator—their cosmic puppet-master. For life to have meaning, God must grant to all rational beings the irrevocable powers of moral discernment and of choice. However, the possessors of this privileged power could potentially abuse it. Any beings who willfully disobeyed would thereby engender a moral crisis beyond their own capacity to solve.

Naturally, the God who created the universe by His word also communicated to every part of it complete and clear instruction in all that pertained to life and godliness (see Psalms 19; 139). Moreover, He generously met the needs of all, leaving no grounds for any to be dissatisfied. No good thing did He withhold from His faithful, loyal creation; daily He loaded all with benefits. God's love is attentive, bountiful, and expressive. Therefore, departure from His stated will could not be an accident but a choice, a deliberate act of ungrateful rebellion and distrust.

The Originator of Rebellion

Lucifer, the highest ranking of God's created beings, the one who stood next to His throne as prime minister of the universe, was the originator of rebellion. Scripture reveals that Lucifer abused his free moral agency not by mistake or under any provocation, but through pride and self-exaltation. God did not plant these seeds of evil; Lucifer was perfect when he was created (see Ezekiel 28:15). He was not the victim of mistreatment, poverty, overwork, or any form of abuse. Rather, God conferred every privilege and honor upon him, and He endowed him with every talent that the most intelligent and enterprising mind could wish. But gradually Lucifer became infatuated with himself. Pride blurred his awareness that all his talents and abilities and his life itself were gifts from his Creator. Eventually he coveted the honor and worship that belong to God alone (see Isaiah 14:13, 14).

Until Lucifer converted his liberty into rebellion, all God's creatures had served God with a pure, cheerful love borne of an appreciation of His character. Their allegiance to Him sprang forth unshadowed by doubt or discontentment. But Lucifer was a cunning communicator. He subtly insinuated his disaffection toward God into the minds of the angels over whose ranks he presided. He expressed his innuendoes concerning God's character so artfully that the angels were perplexed. After all, Lucifer was the premier angel, and the questions he raised seemed plausible: Why do perfect angels need laws of governance when their own inherent wisdom is a sufficient guide? What greater claim to worship did the Son of God have than did Lucifer himself? Indeed, Lucifer's beauty and capabilities did not seem conspicuously inferior to those of the Son.

God clarified the matter before the universe. He plainly identified His Son as co-eternally divine and co-supreme in authority with Himself. He bade all the angels of God to worship Him, not under duress, but because He is the Creator and Sustainer of life (see Hebrews 1:1-8). And the majority of the angels sided with God in the controversy that Lucifer had ignited. Their love for God and loyalty to Him became more deeply rooted when Lucifer's slanderous breath blew its sharp blasts. Despite God's compassionate reasoning with Lucifer and the intercession of angels to persuade him to reconsider his ways, Lucifer progressively hardened himself in rebellion and pride. He wove an ever more intricate web of complaints and charges against God—misrepresentations both subtle and malevolent.

Lucifer's sophistry ensnared a third of the angels. They joined him in sullen resistance to divine counsel, thus shattering the atmosphere of harmony that had previously flourished in heaven. Angels, loyal and disloyal, became engaged in complex theological discussions about God's character and purposes—which had previously never been called into question. Dissension deepened. Two camps were formed, and the gulf between them widened as time passed and the controversy grew.

Eventually, the dissidence that Lucifer implanted in the hearts of the disaffected angels flared into open rebellion. No longer God's light-bearer to the universe, Lucifer was now Satan, the adversary—also called the dragon because of his ugly temper and violent passions. A parting of ways between the loyal and the disloyal became inevitable:

> There was war in heaven: Michael and his angels fought against the dragon; and the dragon fought and his angels, and prevailed not; neither was their place found any more in heaven. And the great dragon was cast out, that old serpent, called the Devil, and Satan, which deceiveth the whole world: he was cast out into the earth, and his angels were cast out with him (Revelation 12:7-9).

God revealed to the faithful angels the price that He would pay to restore moral harmony to the universe. He would not revoke freedom of choice. He would not resort to coercion. He had a better plan. Deep in His heart lay a reserve of love's noblest quality—self-sacrificing mercy. This sovereign remedy for moral revolt and its ensuing disorder would be revealed only if necessity called it forth. God deemed free choice to be so vital that He was willing to pay the cost for its perpetuation while at the same time securing the universe against all future abuse of moral freedom.

"The plan for our redemption was not an afterthought. . . . It was a revelation of 'the mystery which hath been kept in silence through times eternal.' Rom. 16:25, R.V. It was an unfolding of the principles that from eternal ages have been the foundation of God's throne. From the beginning, God and Christ knew of the apostasy of Satan, and of the fall of man through the deceptive power of the apostate. God did not ordain that sin should exist, but He foresaw its existence, and made provision to meet the terrible emergency. So great was His love for the world, that He covenanted to give His only-begotten Son, 'that whosoever believeth in Him should not perish, but have everlasting life.' John 3:16."[1]

The Suffering Commander

By settled commitment as unchanging as divine law and love, Jesus was revealed to unfallen beings throughout the universe as "the Lamb slain from the foundation of the world" (Revelation 13:8). What grief it must have caused the universe to realize the suffering that their beloved Commander would endure for redemption's sake! But recognizing that this sacrifice would ensure the eternal security of the universe, the angels bowed low in reverence before Him. They were willing and eager to assist Him in every way toward the accomplishment of His great design. Their vital participation in carrying out God's plan offered the angels a far deeper education in the mysteries of divine justice and mercy than they could possibly have had if they were mere passive spectators of all His actions (see Psalms 103:19-21; 104:1-4; 68:17; Deuteronomy 33:1-3; Acts 7:53; John 1:51).

God's loyal angels uphold the law and accentuate His overtures of grace. But Lucifer, the sworn enemy of God's law, began by resenting the first commandment, which declares God's unique supremacy and establishes His right to rule. Thus he violated the two fundamental precepts of all the moral law: love to God and love for all His created beings. Lucifer's daring, demented words reflect his hunger for the homage that belongs to God alone: "I will exalt my throne above the stars of God; . . . I will be like the most High" (Isaiah 14:13, 14). This warped and unwarranted craving for worship drove him to ply his energies toward discrediting God and making Him appear unworthy of worship.

Just as Lucifer had deceived the angels by his charming sophistry and insinuation, so he deceived the first woman. A careful analysis of Genesis 3:1-6 exposes the basic methods of deception that he uses to entice humanity to apostasize.

1. He assumed a disguise.
2. He asked a question designed to raise doubts about God and the reliability of His word.
3. He implied that God was arbitrarily restrictive.
4. He denied that disobedience to God's word would result in any adverse consequences.
5. He denied the reality of death, implying that its prospect was an empty threat of a tyrannical and impotent god.
6. He said that disobedience to God's word was the path to a liberation that would enable the latent divinity of human beings to blossom independent of any external divine authority.
7. He implied that evil was a more advanced form of good that God was jealously withholding to keep human beings blindly under His dominion.
8. And he implied that human powers of observation and judgment were superior to any divinely revealed instructions or warnings.

This is Satan's eight-fold path to ultimate ruin. All false religion and philosophy offers endless variations on this octave of beguiling sophistries.

Eve capitulated to Satan's lies, and Adam, prizing her supremely, followed her example. Having cast away their garments of light, they now stood naked, shivering in the chilly air of insubordination to

God's loving will and flight from His fellowship. Their venture into psychedelic indulgence left them frightened, bleary, and degraded. But God did not abandon our first parents. He drew them forth from their quivering fear and shame and their vain hiding place, and He clothed them with substantial garments that represented the covering of His grace and the glory of His plan.

Adam and Eve could not transmit to their offspring anything but their now-fallen nature, but God revealed that His grace is sufficient to subdue humanity's inborn corruption and implant His regenerating righteousness in all who will accept it. His plan ensures the redemption of their souls and the eventual annihilation of all evil and its dread effects. It reveals that until the battle against good and evil is finally and fully resolved on this stage of action called earth, the whole planet and all its inhabitants will be enveloped in an atmosphere of grace charged with opportunities and providences, with revelations and influences to maximize each person's prospect of redemption.

With magnificent compactness of thought, Romans 5 expounds the theology of God's epic intervention. Indeed, all Scripture unfolds redemption's story in a continuous panorama of preserved history and sure prophecy. Whether we accept or reject salvation, each individual life attests to the reality of God's labors of love to turn defeat and disgrace into glorious restoration for this sin-ravaged race.

---

1. Ellen G. White, *The Desire of Ages* (Nampa, Idaho: Pacific Press®, 1940), 22.

Luminous Shadows of His Sacrifice

An Englishman who had become a citizen of the United States went to Cuba at the outbreak of that country's revolution in 1867. He was arrested on suspicion of spying and condemned to be shot. Both the British and the American consuls strove for the man's release, but they were unsuccessful.

On the day this man was to be executed, he was brought out of prison, carried in a cart to his freshly dug grave, and a black hood was placed over his head. As the firing squad raised their guns, the British and American consuls rushed forward and spread the flags of their countries over the condemned man. Knowing that orders to fire would effectively declare war on the two nations whose flags draped his prisoner, the Spanish captain quietly lowered his sword and looked away. Without interference, the two consuls conducted the man to safety and arranged for his return home.

Two flags secure *our* safety from eternal destruction—the word and the blood of Christ that wrap us in a pledge of redemption. God's Spirit enfolds us in these two banners, the insignia of our calling (see 1 John 5:4-13).

Ever since Adam's fall, it has been God's chief aim to restore sinful humanity to oneness with Himself and to eradicate evil. He accomplishes this aim by means of His atonement, which down through the ages has extended marvelous protection to us all, even to the rebellious.

Long before the Cross, the Lord revealed His plan of redemption in types and symbols designed to enlighten humanity and to sensitize all people to the exceeding evil of sin and to the fathomless depths of the love that moved Him to bear the high cost of our salvation. Unless we understand why sin is such a problem, we won't ascribe much importance to the plan of salvation. It will seem like an overwrought exercise in moral theatrics.

Scripture defines sin as both transgression of the law and willful disharmony with God (1 John 3:4; Nehemiah 9:26-29). Sin is not an entertaining alternative to righteousness; it is the enemy of truth, the antithesis of love, the negation of life. It stands implacably opposed to everything that gives grace, virtue, and beauty to our existence. It drives its slaves into stubborn, rebellious darkness and a determination to quench the light of truth (see John 3:19, 20; Ephesians 5:6-13).

Sin deceives and hardens the heart, deadening the "nerve endings" of our conscience. It is a spiritual cancer that destroys the essential health and happiness of our whole being. Its influence is degrading, its character aggressive, its movement relentless, its action destructive, its legacy shame, its wages death. Worst of all, it strikes out at God with ruthless hostility. It separates and alienates us from Him (see Isaiah 59:1, 2; Ephesians 4:18). And all of us are by nature infected with this morally fatal virus (see Romans 3:10-12, 23). It must be eradicated, for it damages everything it touches and destroys everything it controls.

Sin, then, is not a game nor a viable alternative to holiness. This might seem too obvious to mention, but if so, why does the world make a joke of it (see Proverbs 10:23; 14:9), as if it were the spice of life and a species of entertainment? Sinful behavior rather than uprightness of character and conduct is the stock theme of most popular songs, books, and plays, and of much everyday conversation.

One of sin's most blinding effects is its tendency to prevent people from recognizing God as our Creator and to lead them to believe instead that we are self-existent and naturally immortal (see Romans

1:18-32). But we are totally dependent for our existence on God, who created us in His own image.

A Promised Son

After Adam and Eve's banishment from the Garden of Eden, they maintained their contact with God through worship that looked to the promised Son who would crush the serpent's (Satan's) head at the cost of great suffering to Himself (see Genesis 3:15). Scripture doesn't elaborate on the system of sacrifices that Adam and Eve practiced. But it does clearly indicate that the sacrifice of lambs as an expression of repentance and faith in the coming Messiah was central to worship from the time of the Fall. It was Cain's pride and his rejection of his need of a Savior that kept him from offering the sacrifice God had specifically designated. Thus he rejected the gospel of salvation by grace (see Genesis 4:1-8; Hebrews 11:4; 1 John 3:11-15).

"Cain came before God with murmuring and infidelity in his heart in regard to the promised sacrifice and the necessity of the sacrificial offerings. His gift expressed no penitence for sin. He felt, as many now feel, that it would be an acknowledgment of weakness to follow the exact plan marked out by God, of trusting his salvation wholly to the atonement of the promised Saviour. He chose the course of self-dependence. He would come in his own merits. He would not bring the lamb, and mingle its blood with his offering, but would present *his* fruits, the products of *his* labor. He presented his offering as a favor done to God. . . . Cain obeyed in building an altar, obeyed in bringing a sacrifice; but . . . the essential part, the recognition of the need of a Redeemer, was left out."[1]

Cain exemplified the universal principle of false religion—that humans can bypass the atonement and depend on their own efforts for salvation. Cain "felt good about himself," to use the modern catchphrase, so what need did he have to repent? Yes, he would worship God, but on his own terms. Cain might thank God for His bounties, but he would acknowledge no guilt, no need for a new heart, no need for the Lamb. Beneath his veneer of suave piety lurked the pride and anger that drove him to kill his brother, whose gentle entreaties to offer the divinely required lamb were an affront to Cain's self-esteem. Here we see the fundamental intolerance toward the gospel that rankles in sin-loving hearts. Cain's behavior typifies the world's treatment of Jesus and His followers, who worship Him in spirit and in truth.

It has always been true that only a remnant is responsive to God's purposes. While the rest of the world abandoned itself to iniquity and violence, Noah and his family worshiped God on His terms. Noah's first act upon leaving the ark after the flood waters resided was to offer sacrifices to the Lord (see Genesis 8:20). And true to the world's pattern of succumbing to Satan's deceptions, the majority of Noah's descendants, though not all, tumbled into apostate religion and idolatry (see Genesis 11). Then God called Abraham, whose heart was inclined to Him, to be the progenitor of the faithful. He led him from Ur of the Chaldees to Canaan, where, removed from heathen influence, he and his family could cultivate a deeper and purer relationship with God (see Genesis 12-14).

God revealed to Abraham the glory of the sacrifice He would make (see Genesis 15:1-17[2]). Abram's walk through the divided halves of the animals sacrificed symbolized the means by which all may gain access to God. He revealed to Abraham that the Messiah's cross was the thoroughfare to redemption, the causeway of grace that stretches from heaven to earth.

Paul wrote that the gospel was preached to Abraham (see Galatians 3:8). This is neither an anachronism nor a fanciful view. For all whose hearts have craved truth, the everlasting gospel has illuminated all the ages of earth's history. Abraham is called the father of the faithful (see Romans 4:11; Galatians 3:7) not because he was genetically superior or because God arbitrarily favored him, but because he opened his heart to the Lord and the glory of His sacrifice.

God favored Abraham in his later years with the most poignant symbolic revelation of Calvary ever entrusted to mortals. He bade him to sacrifice his only son, his promised heir (see Genesis 22:1-14). Scripture reveals that Abraham's faith in God's power to raise his son from the dead braced him to obey this dark summons (see Hebrews 11:17-19).

As Abraham and Isaac slowly climbed Mount Moriah, Isaac, in puzzlement, asked, "Behold the fire and the wood: but where is the lamb for a burnt offering?" Abraham's reply, "My son, God will provide Himself a lamb for a burnt offering," revealed his grasp of the gospel. And Isaac's cooperation with his father's mysterious mission reveals the depth of his spiritual perception and commitment to God.

In this enacted allegory of faith, God was not establishing a precedent for human sacrifices. Rather, He was vividly illustrating the paramount gospel truth that in the fullness of time He would allow His only begotten Son to die for the sins of the world. Before Abraham could consummate the sacrifice, God commanded him to stop. Then He directed Abraham to a ram entangled in a thicket; God had provided that ram as a sacrifice in Isaac's stead.

To commemorate the marvelous occurrences of that day, Abraham named the place on Mount Moriah where these things had happened *Jehovah-jireh*. *Moriah* means "God will instruct," and *Jehovah-jireh* conveys the dual meaning "the Lord will see" and "the Lord will provide."

What could be more instructive than these gospel lessons from God Himself? What reveals His perceptive powers and wisdom more amply than the plan of redemption? What greater provision could He have made than His only begotten Son?

Almost one millennium later, the temple at Jerusalem was built on Moriah (see 2 Chronicles 3:1)—near Calvary. These concurrences of location and events reveal the clarity and continuity of the divine purpose. Calvary has always been imbedded in the core of God's heart.

Out of Bondage

From Abraham sprang the Hebrew nation. Resistant though they were—even as the so-called Christian world is today with its truncated and flesh-pleasing reinterpretation of the truth (see Hebrews 2:4; Luke 18:1)—God guided the Israelites by the light of the gospel. Although God had provided clear and miraculous evidence that, through Moses, He was leading them from bondage to the Promised Land, they murmured almost incessantly against Moses' leadership because of the hardships along the way. Their turbulent, ungrateful spirit provided greenhouse conditions for the growth of trials and miseries (see Exodus 14:10-14; 15:22-24; 16:2-4; cp. 1 Corinthians 10:10-13).

God hadn't concealed His presence from them, nor did He withhold His love or His truth. He who has declared Himself to be abundant in goodness, truth, and mercy daily loaded them with benefits. But a veil of unbelief covered their hearts, obscuring the glory of God's character and purpose. Thus they made life a wasteland and a drudgery for themselves, when it could have been a land of living streams and radiant joy.

Sin has infected the human race with Satan's own petulant, surly disposition. God's love often makes its way into our lives through a tortuous obstacle course that we construct out of the craggy materials of discontent and unbelief. Satan tempts us to treat God as an equal or an inferior whom we must punish from time to time for the way He treats us. All too dimly do we realize how this peevishness wounds others, blinds our own hearts, and deadens our love for God.

Only a few days after the Israelites passed miraculously through the Red Sea, they accused Moses and Aaron of bringing them out into the wilderness to starve. In another unprecedented miracle, the Lord rained manna from the sky for their daily sustenance. Then they complained that God was not providing them with drinking water, and, in their irrational rage, they considered stoning Moses for luring them into the wilderness to die. Instead of punishing this throng of mutinous refugees for their perverse unbelief, God directed Moses to smite a giant rock in Horeb. When he did, fresh water flowed in abundance, meeting their needs (see Exodus 17:1-7; Psalm 78:15-17).

These historic events convey important gospel lessons (see John 7:37-39; 1 Corinthians 10:1; Isaiah 11:9; 12:3, 4; 32:1, 2). Jesus is the smitten Rock from whom flows the water of life. God wishes us to drink abundantly of His life, that we may be conduits through which He can dispense the water of life to irrigate this spiritually parched world. From our hearts, our homes, our churches, and our communities He longs to see "justice run down like water, and righteousness like a mighty stream" (Amos 5:24, NKJV).

We live after the Cross and Pentecost. How much further advanced should be our faith and fidelity than was that of ancient Israel![3] God wants our lives to be a standing invitation that declares in word and action, "Let him that is athirst come. And whosoever will, let him take the water of life freely" (Revelation 22:17). To do this, we must exercise the spirit of hospitality and benevolence often. Let's drink of Jesus so that rivers of living water will flow from our inmost being (see Zechariah 13:1; John 19:33-35; 1 John 5:4-8).

Moses' example punctuates the lesson that those who love God and long to see His cause honored in the church must be patient and longsuffering. If, in the interests of promoting reform, we chide God's people, may we not be smiting the rock? May we not be usurping God's authority to chasten and correct the erring (see Numbers 20:9-13; Psalm 106:32, 33; Hebrews 12:13-15; 1 Peter 1:14-21)? God's servants must declare His whole counsel, but we must do so with meekness and godly fear, lest we obscure the glory of God's character and exhibit instead the self-righteous harshness of Satan (see 2 Timothy 2:24-26).

During Israel's long sojourn in the wilderness, God in mercy had miraculously protected them from the fiery serpents and scorpions teeming there. He had preserved their health and vitality and given them water and nutritious food in abundance, as well as guidance on their journey and protection from hostile tribes. Still, the people as a whole seethed with discontent. At the root of it all was resentment against God's holy calling for them as a nation (see Psalm 78:10, 11, 33-42). They had no more pleasure in His truth than they did in the manna, which they regarded as insubstantial and insipid. While their feet were moving circuitously toward the Promised Land, their hearts were steadily moving toward perdition. Though the gospel was preached to them, few benefited from it because they did not receive it in faith.

Venomous Serpents

To awaken the people to their ultimate danger, God withdrew His protecting hand for a brief period and allowed the venomous serpents to dart out of their hiding places. Their lethal bite struck down many Israelites. Now the people were aroused to a sense of their sins and unjust complaints. God directed Moses to cast a bronze serpent and raise it upon a pole. All the victims of snakebite who cast a look of faith toward this symbol were miraculously healed (see Numbers 21:4-8).

"They knew that there was no virtue in the serpent itself, but it was a symbol of Christ; and the necessity of faith in His merits was thus presented to their minds. . . . So the sinner may look to Christ, and live. He receives pardon through faith in the atoning sacrifice. Unlike the inert and lifeless symbol, Christ has power and virtue in Himself to heal the repenting sinner."[4]

Jesus explained to Nicodemus that this bronze serpent fore-shadowed His own sacrifice on Calvary (see John 3:14-16). What an amazing image—that Jesus should be cast as the devil, that He should die at the hands of the devil the very death that this vile serpent of serpents deserves. Jesus died for us who are so devilish at heart; He died so that by the antivenom of His grace He might transform us into saints and make us partakers of His divine nature. While this exchange was royally merciful to us, it was brutally unfair to God. Yet God offers it to us out of a heart of willing love. He is not bitter about its cost. Let us sweetly accept it without doubt or cold reserve. Let us look to Jesus, the Author and Finisher of our faith, who for the joy set before Him endured the Cross, despising the shame. Let us look and live!

When the Israelites of old began to idolize the bronze serpent that for centuries had been kept in the sanctuary, King Hezekiah destroyed it (see 2 Kings 18:1-6). It is not the cross itself that we are to revere, but the crucified and risen Savior. May the Lord give us grace to distinguish between a sentimental adoration of the cross and a genuine response to the One who was delivered for our offenses and raised again for our justification, the One who bore our sins in His own body on the tree that we, being dead to sin, might live unto righteousness.

The Old Testament holds many foregleams of the Cross besides those we have considered here. For example, the service by which Israel prepared for their exodus from bondage set before them an open door into the glorious realm of the gospel, emphasizing the need of wholehearted reliance on Jesus' blood—as did the sprinkling of the book and of the people at Sinai and as did the cities of refuge from avengers of blood (see Exodus 12:1-28; 24:1-8; Numbers 35:11-32; Deuteronomy 19:1-13). The plan of salvation runs like a scarlet thread throughout all the types, rituals, and customs of ancient Hebrew life and worship. Christ and His saving sacrifice comprise the key that unlocks the mysteries of the Old Testament. They sound the keynote of its sacred harmony, and they form the keystone of the bridge that connects the ages of divine revelation from Paradise lost to Paradise regained.

From the gates of Eden, God progressively unfolded the plan of salvation that informs humanity that Jesus, the sacrificial Lamb, is the one avenue to redemption. Despite all the obstacles of willful ignorance and satanic opposition, this revelation shone with growing distinctness and gathering brightness from age to age until it blazed forth in all its power on Calvary.

---

1. Ellen G. White, *Patriarchs and Prophets* (Nampa, Idaho: Pacific Press®, 1958), 72; see also pp. 71–77.

2. See also ibid., 137.

3. See ibid., 414–421.

4. Ibid., 430, 431.

Prophetic Profiles
of Calvary

Solomon Ginsburg, raised in a devout Jewish home and showing great promise as a rabbinic student, fled his native Poland to avoid a prearranged marriage. At seventeen, alone and friendless in London, he accepted a young Jewish missionary's invitation to hear a lecture about the Messiah. Solomon listened electrified as the speaker explained Isaiah 53 verse by verse. He recalled the day four years prior when he sat at a Succoth feast with his rabbi father and read through that chapter in thoughtful silence. He had asked his father, "Of whom does the prophet speak here?" His father's forbidding reply had intensified Solomon's determination to understand this hauntingly beautiful portion of Scripture.

In that London lecture hall, the answer came to Solomon as he saw Jesus presented with piercing clarity in sacred words written hundreds of years before His birth. That night Solomon received Jesus as his Messiah. Soon afterward he became a lifelong missionary to Brazil. With dauntless energy, courage, and zeal, he led thousands to Jesus along a pathway of witness ablaze with the glory of the Cross whose first rays had shone upon him from Isaiah's prophetic depiction.

Calvary shines brilliantly through the ancient word of prophecy. Nothing about Jesus' future sacrifice was obscure in God's mind. Clear about its need, nature, timing, cost, and everlasting results, God made the Messiah's redeeming sacrifice the focal point of Israel's system of worship, laws, and prophecies. All the ancient signboards are painted with the luminescent ink of Jesus' blood. They glow in the deepest darkness of earth's apostasy and shame, sending out the message, "This is the way, walk in it; for the path of My Son's sacrifice is the way to Eden restored."

To use another metaphor, the backlights of the Old Testament projected the glory of the Cross onto the screen of events then future but now accomplished. In it we see that Jesus truly is "the Lamb slain from the foundation of the world" (Revelation 13:8). God's all-pervading message, whether in the types and prophecies of the Old Testament or the narratives and doctrines of the New, is "I love you and gave Myself for you, to meet all your needs."

Salvation from sin is our greatest need. Accordingly, God revealed to Israel a system of worship designed to bridge the gulf sin had forged between Him and humanity. He said to Israel, "Let them make me a sanctuary; that I may dwell among them" (Exodus 25:8). On Mount Sinai, God showed Moses the pattern of the sanctuary and all its furnishings (see Exodus 25:9, 40). Nothing so vital to human development and destiny could be left to unreliable human imagination.

The Gospel in Metaphor

Every aspect of the sanctuary and its services presented the gospel in a living metaphor. David sang, "In his temple, everything saith, Glory" (Psalm 29:9, ASV). God expressed His desire not only to redeem humanity from sin but also to beautify His people with His goodness and holiness, so that they, as the temple of God, might live to His glory and reveal Him attractively to others.

God employed simple but graphic means to accomplish this end. He instructed repentant sinners to bring a kid or lamb to the sanctuary for a sin offering (see Leviticus 4:27-34). Never done under duress, the supplicants' action signified their faith in the atoning virtue of the coming Messiah's sacrifice and their personal appropriation of the benefit. Before taking the life of the lamb, they confessed their sins over the spotless, innocent creature. Both the sacrifice and the presiding priest represented the Messiah (see John 1:29; Hebrews

7:20-28). The priests presented morning and evening sacrifices, which represented God's universal mercies that enable all who so desire to be saved (see Exodus 29:38, 39; 1 John 2:2; cp. Exodus 12:48, 49; 1 Kings 8:41-43). All the lessons taught in the earthly tabernacle mirrored in miniature the sanctuary in heaven, which the Lord constructed and not man. Truly, as the psalmist declared, "Thy way, O God, is in the sanctuary" (Psalm 77:13).

God honored the sanctuary with His presence in the form of a visible light to bless His people and accept the services they performed there (see Exodus 40:33-38). Jesus, the Light of the world, became flesh and tabernacled among us to reveal the glory and grace of God and the truth of His ways. He became our living sanctuary, the open treasure house of redemption, righteousness, sanctification, and wisdom (see John 1:14).

Every worshiper who engaged in the sanctuary services with thoughtful reverence recognized that the animal offerings were not an adequate symbol of what the Lord Himself was bearing for the sake of our salvation. Only the advent of the divine-human Sin Bearer could complete the picture. The tabernacle services stood as a perpetual prophecy of the Messiah to come (see Hebrews 9:11-16, 24-26).

Summarizing the prophets' view of this matter, Peter wrote,

> Of this salvation the prophets have inquired and searched diligently, who prophesied of the grace that would come to you, searching what, or what manner of time, the Spirit of Christ who was in them was indicating when He testified beforehand the sufferings of Christ and the glories that would follow. To them it was revealed that, not to themselves, but to us they were ministering the things which now have been reported to you through those who have preached the gospel to you by the Holy Spirit sent from heaven—things which angels desire to look into* (1 Peter 1:10-12, NKJV).

---

* The angels' fascination with the marvels and mysteries of redemption was represented in the sculpture of the tabernacle by their reverent gaze toward the mercy seat (see Exodus 25:16-21).

God's covenant is ordered in all things, and sure, omitting no needed lesson or provision for our souls. At their root, the ancient sanctuary services of Israel presented the new covenant in a pageant of symbols that eloquently declared in tongues of fire:

> [Behold] the Lamb [of God] slain from the foundation of the world (Revelation 13:8).
> The life of the flesh is in the blood: and I have given it to you upon the altar to make an atonement for your souls: for it is the blood that maketh an atonement for the soul (Leviticus 17:11).
> Without shedding of blood is no remission (Hebrews 9:22).
> This is my blood of the new testament [covenant], which is shed for many for the remission of sins (Matthew 26:28).

A Prophecy of the Gospel

We have seen that the sanctuary services formed a prophecy of the gospel in allegorical ceremonies that God Himself prescribed. For further illumination, He gave specific prophecies concerning the Messiah's coming. In these prophecies the Messiah's travail and sacrifice are etched in clear, explicit lines as lucid and detailed as an eyewitness account.

Consider, for example, Psalm 22, which spotlights the events of Calvary as though they were occurring in our presence. We note

- Jesus' cry of anguish and dereliction from the cross; His being treated as a worm rather than as a man
- the reproach and derision heaped upon Him
- the very words of taunting and defiance that the Pharisees used as they watched Him suffer
- the desertion of His friends
- the roaring mob that surrounded His cross
- the incessant volley of vile accusations that were bellowed in His face as He hung suspended between heaven and earth
- His being painfully stretched out, with enormous strain on every joint and fiber of His body
- His intense thirst

- His pierced hands and feet
- His nakedness
- the division of and gambling for His garments

In Psalm 22 we feel the heaving in Jesus' chest as He labored for each breath and the pain that gored every nerve, caused by the spikes that riveted Him to the rough beams of wood. We feel the clutch of His searing thirst as the sap of life drained away. Yet for all its vividness, this psalm is significantly more than a prophetic tableau of Jesus' crucifixion. It reveals to thoughtful readers the very core of Jesus' soul as He looked upon the turbulent sea of blasphemous onlookers that surged around the cross. In it we sense, however dimly, the abysmal grief and palpable darkness that engulfed Him as He bore the full penalty for our transgressions and became "sin for us, who knew no sin; that we might be made the righteousness of God in him" (2 Corinthians 5:21). Jesus foresaw Himself plunging into the chasm of perdition where Satan and his followers belong. He foresaw it all, but did not refuse it.

What a contrast between darkness and light appears in Psalm 22! From the crucified Messiah's measureless grief while He is swathed in dense clouds of pain and rejection (verses 1-21), we are swept into the shining atmosphere of Calvary triumphant and all that it means for our salvation and the final conquest of evil (verses 22-31).

Isaiah 53 is the second crown jewel of Messianic prophecy. This chapter and Psalm 22 rise like the two pillars in the porch of Solomon's temple—Jachin and Boaz (see 1 Kings 7:21, 22). *Jachin* means "he shall establish," and *Boaz*, "in it is strength." The cross of Calvary established the strength of the plan of salvation, a strength that nothing can overthrow; a strength that makes invincible the weakest sinner who relies solely on Jesus' saving grace.

The last part of Isaiah 52 and chapter 53 encapsulate the whole gospel. Isaiah's beautiful presentation of the Savior and His redeeming work emphasizes that the small portion of humanity that does accept the Messiah's salvation will be God's ultimate satisfaction and reward (see Isaiah 53:11; cp. Hebrews 12:2; 1 Thessalonians 2:19).

One can't help being struck by Isaiah 53's depiction of the world's fierce rejection of the Messiah. Why this firestorm of malice against the

One who is the Soul of tact, the Fountainhead of mercy, the Prince of peace, the King of love, the Incarnation of grace? He wasn't abrasive, aloof, or unkind toward anyone. Rather, He "went about doing good" (Acts 10:38). But people, especially religious people, felt condemned by the purity of His life. Not that He projected a "holier than thou" attitude. He simply was the living embodiment of divine righteousness—a righteousness that He invited all to receive by means of His grace.

However, the people preferred their rituals to His righteousness, their pageantry to the power that could make them pure and free. So they clung to their foul rags of false godliness and formed a lynching party, a Passover parade to slay the sacrificial Lamb on Calvary with bloodthirsty glee. In heart, people repeat this process from generation to generation by clothing themselves in the threadbare garments of their own delusions, their own customized code of "spiritual" beliefs. Their experience, described in Isaiah 64:6, Romans 10:3, and Revelation 3:17, contrasts starkly with the condition of those who reject all self-made imitations and accept instead the true righteousness of God (see Romans 3:21-26; Philippians 3:7-9; Revelation 19:7-10). "Let no one take the limited, narrow position that any of the works of man can help in the least possible way to liquidate the debt of his transgression. This is a fatal deception. If you would understand it, you must . . . with humble hearts survey the atonement."[1]

The Dominant Chord of Isaiah 53

As we trace the line of thought in Isaiah 53, we see a rich emphasis on the substitutionary and expiatory nature of Jesus' sacrifice for all humanity. It is the dominant chord throughout. This theme, which is steadily developed in Isaiah, not only highlights God's merciful love, it also explodes the notion that "good works" can do anything to atone for sin or secure salvation (see Isaiah 26:12, 13; 27:2-6; 40:1-11; 45:22-25; 54:11-17; 61:1-3, 10, 11; 63:7-9; 64:4-8). Isaiah 53 "should be studied. It presents Christ as the Lamb of God. Those who are lifted up with pride, whose souls are filled with vanity, should look upon this picture of their Redeemer, and humble themselves in the dust. The entire chapter should be committed to memory. Its influence will subdue and humble the soul defiled by sin and uplifted by self-exaltation."[2]

The Father declared, "By his knowledge shall my righteous servant justify many; for he shall bear their iniquities" and make "intercession for the transgressors" (Isaiah 53:11, 12). What sort of "knowledge" is required to justify humans who, through sin, are in a naturally unjustified state of being? As we seek the answer, we can only declare, "Oh the depth of the riches both of the wisdom and knowledge of God! how unsearchable are his judgments, and his ways past finding out!" (Romans 11:33). If we knew how much God loves us and how exalted are the purposes of His love, that realization would transform our whole outlook on life. We would do well to ponder this theme as set forth in Romans 5:16-21.

What response can this realization of God's care awaken in our hearts other than that we turn to look and live? Zechariah prophetically captured the transcendent effects of Calvary on receptive hearts.

> I will pour upon the house of David, and upon the inhabitants of Jerusalem, the spirit of grace and supplications: and they shall look upon me whom they have pierced, and they shall mourn for him, as one mourneth for his only son, and shall be in bitterness for him, as one that is in bitterness for his firstborn. . . . In that day there shall be a fountain opened to the house of David and to the inhabitants of Jerusalem for sin and for uncleanness (Zechariah 12:10; 13:1).

And Paul wrote:

> Not by works of righteousness which we have done, but according to his mercy he saved us, by the washing of regeneration, and renewing of the Holy Ghost; which he shed on us abundantly through Jesus Christ our Saviour; that being justified by his grace, we should be made heirs according to the hope of eternal life (Titus 3:5-7).

Calvary is the searchlight that awakens the conscience; it is the crucible that purifies the soul. "The purity, the holiness, of the life of Jesus as presented from the Word of God possess more power to reform and transform the character than do all the efforts put forth in picturing sins and crimes of men and the sure results. One steadfast look to the Saviour uplifted upon the cross will do more to purify the mind and heart from every defilement than will all the scientific explanations by the ablest tongue."[3]

The Bible's Greatest Time Prophecy

It is of high significance that the greatest time prophecy in the Bible—Daniel 9:24-27 linked with Daniel 8:14—converges on Calvary and the glorious effects of that sacrifice, which transcend time and encompass eternity. This coronating Messianic prophecy clearly portrays the Cross as the moral axis of the universe. Messiah shall be cut off "to make an end of sins, and to make reconciliation for iniquity, and to bring in everlasting righteousness, and to seal up the vision and prophecy" (Daniel 9:24).

Several hundred additional prophecies bearing on the Messiah paint a portrait that makes His identity unmistakably clear. Any contender for Messiahship would have to be born of a virgin in Bethlehem of Davidic lineage, be baptized and sacrificed at prophetically designated times, appear while the second temple stood, have a forerunner with a definite message and mission, live a morally flawless life, heal the sick, open blind eyes, cast out demons, preach the gospel to the poor, be betrayed by a friend for thirty pieces of silver, suffer the desertion of his disciples, be crucified with criminals, buried in a rich man's tomb, rise the third day, ascend to heaven, and launch an immortal, worldwide movement based on his own life and teachings.

No impostor could assume this role in the face of so many definitive and confluent tests, for which only the overruling providence of God could provide fulfillment. This was why Jesus, after He arose, presented so many scriptural evidences of His identity to the apostles (see Luke 24:17-27, 44, 45). "It is the light from the prophetic past that brings out the life of Christ and the teachings of the New Testament with clearness and beauty. The miracles of Christ are a proof of His divinity; but a stronger proof that He is the world's Redeemer is found in comparing the prophecies of the Old Testament with the history of the New."[4]

Calvary is the guiding light of the ages that penetrates the thickest fog and reaches the most desperately storm-tossed of lives whose hearts are open to the radiant beams of redeeming grace. In his autobiography, William Grenfell relates an experience that poignantly exemplifies in a minor key this glorious truth.

Dr. Grenfell and a colleague came to a fishing village on an island off the Labrador coast. On arriving they found a young woman suffering from typhoid. Cook and housekeeper for a band of fishermen, she was now, at eighteen, stricken with fatal illness. Grenfell's exertions on her behalf served only to make her death a little less agonizing. While he strove to help her, several of the fishermen, all brothers, went to sea. The woman died while they fished. After gently placing her body in a rude pine coffin, Grenfell, as a hygienic measure, gathered up her clothes, mattress, and few belongings, took them down to the beach, and burned them. The blaze of this bonfire mounted like a brilliant spire in the sharp night air.

Meanwhile, Grenfell and the fishermen's father grew increasingly anxious about the still-absent crew. It was now dark and blustery, and a thick fog had rolled in. Shortly after the melancholy incineration of the young woman's meager possessions, the fishing party landed and returned to their hut. They had been completely lost in the thick fog, but the bonfire on the shore enabled them to get their bearings. Its blaze, penetrating the fog, provided them with just enough light so they could make their way to safety.

This story is a pale illustration of the luminous power of the Cross, which throughout all ages has emitted steady streams of light that have guided to God's safe shore multitudes who were struggling on life's tempestuous sea. God's Spirit and angels give stimulus and efficiency to our feeble efforts to pull the oars toward home. He provides the grace that is greater than all our sin, grace that is mightier than all our fears, all our foes, and all our failures, if only we put our trust in Him.

1. Ellen G. White, *Our High Calling* (Hagerstown, Md.: Review and Herald, 1961), 122.
2. Ellen G. White, *Youth's Instructor*, December 20, 1900, 394.
3. Ellen G. White, *Lift Him Up* (Hagerstown, Md.: Review and Herald, c.1951), 297.
4. Ellen G. White, *The Desire of Ages* (Nampa, Idaho: Pacific Press®, 1940), 799.

CHAPTER 4

Great Is the Mystery
of Godliness

Two theologians debated over the nature of Christ, each tenaciously holding to his own view and insisting that the other's view was sacrilegious. Finally, after weeks of wrangling, they visited, together, an eminent Bible scholar whom they both respected. After presenting their cases to him, one of the disputants asked, "Dr. ———, what nature did Christ possess?" Looking at their troubled faces, he replied, "Just how Jesus' human nature blended with and remained distinct from His divine, just how He was tempted in all points like as we are while at the same time having no propensity toward sin as we do—we must wait until heaven for Him to reveal these things more fully to us. Until then I rest on the conviction that Jesus was enough like me to be my Savior, and enough unlike me not to need a Savior. Meanwhile, would it not glorify Him if this great mystery of God had such influence in our lives as to give us a spirit of brotherly kindness and mutual regard even if we do not see everything about it identically?"

What Christ, the ever-living God, achieved in His humanity is the key to our redemption. Knowing this, Satan has provoked many to make the Incarnation, the great "mystery of godliness," a subject of strife and debate. But Christ is not divided, and He certainly doesn't wish His people to array in battle formation against one another over so sacred a theme. It would be far better for us to enter this holy ground on bended knee—as did the shepherds at Bethlehem—rather than with an avenging sword, intent on smiting those with contrary views.

It is ill-advised to make our convictions regarding the nature of Christ a test of others' Christian experience (see Romans 14:4, 8-13).* Scripture not only forbids us to judge others, it also warns us that there are divine mysteries beyond our understanding:

> Without controversy great is the mystery of godliness: God was manifest in the flesh, justified in the Spirit, seen of angels, preached unto the Gentiles, believed on in the world, received up into glory (1 Timothy 3:16).

> O the depth of the riches both of the wisdom and knowledge of God! how unsearchable are his judgments, and his ways past finding out! For who hath known the mind of the Lord? or who hath been his counsellor? . . . For of him, and through him, and to him, are all things: to whom be glory for ever. Amen (Romans 11:33, 34, 36).

Paul's Spirit-quickened grasp of the Incarnation and atonement made his pen the conduit of much information about this subject. While he did not profess to understand fully the inner workings of the Incarnation, yet he knew that everything about it was wonderful and adapted to our redemption without artifice or inadequacy.

Why, Not How

Regarding Jesus' incarnation, Scripture primarily discloses the *reasons for it,* and has little to say on how His divine and human nature were combined. Consider, for example, the words of Paul: "You, who once were alienated and enemies in your mind by wicked works, yet now has He *reconciled in the body of His flesh through death,* to present you holy, and blameless, and above reproach in His sight" (Colossians 1:21, 22, NKJV; emphasis supplied). This passage states the essential purpose of Jesus' incarnation: He came to offer Himself as a redeeming sacrifice for fallen humanity. He came as our all-effectual Sin

---

* For Ellen G. White's strong warning regarding one's views on the nature of Christ, see note 1 at the end of this chapter.

Bearer and Restorer. "When He came into the world, He said: 'Sacrifice and offering You did not desire, but a body You have prepared for Me. . . . Then I said, "Behold, I have come . . . to do Your will, O God." ' . . . By that will we have been sanctified through the offering of the body of Jesus Christ once for all" (Hebrews 10:5, 7, 10, NKJV).

"The Saviour has purchased the fallen race with His own blood. This is a great mystery, a mystery that will not be fully, completely understood in its greatness until the translation of the redeemed shall take place. . . . But the enemy is determined that this gift shall be so mystified that it will become as nothingness. . . .

"The most gifted men on the earth could all find abundant employment, from now until the judgment, for all their God-given powers in exalting the character of Christ. But they would still fail to present Him as He is. The mysteries of redemption, embracing Christ's divine-human character, His incarnation, His atonement for sin, could employ the pens and the highest mental powers of the wisest men from now until Christ shall be revealed in the clouds of heaven in power and great glory. But though these men should seek with all their power to give a representation of Christ and His work, the representation would fall far short of the reality."[2]

Jesus "was made of the seed of David, according to the flesh" (Romans 1:3). "God sending his own Son in the likeness of sinful flesh, and for sin, condemned sin in the flesh: that the righteousness of the law might be fulfilled in us, who walk not after the flesh, but after the Spirit" (Romans 8:3, 4). Jesus condemned sin in the flesh, making it possible for us to live—by His Spirit—free from sin.

While Scripture clearly says that Jesus, for the sake of our salvation, took upon Himself our human nature, even in the diminished state that resulted from Adam's fall, it is equally clear that in one vital respect His human nature differed from ours: He had no inborn bent to evil, as we all do. Here's the paradox: He took our nature debilitated as it was by sin, yet His character and inclinations suffered not the slightest taint of sin. Again we ask, *why* did He come so close to our condition? In Hebrews 2:13-18 we discover that He took our humanity to destroy the power of the devil, deliver us from the bondage of sin and death, make reconciliation for our sins, and strengthen us for victory over all temptation.

38

By virtue of His atoning sacrifice, He is now our High Priest in heaven. No longer subject to death, He's working out the saving counsels of His will to make us subjects of immortality. "He, because He continues forever, has an unchangeable priesthood. Therefore He is also able to save to the uttermost those who come to God through Him, since He ever lives to make intercession for them. For such a High Priest was fitting for us, who is holy, harmless, undefiled, separate from sinners, and has become higher than the heavens; who does not need daily, as those high priests, to offer up sacrifices, first for His own sins and then for the people's, for this He did once for all when He offered up Himself" (Hebrews 7:24-27, NKJV).

Jesus' supernatural conception in Mary's womb by the Holy Spirit was in fulfillment of the age-old prophecy that "a virgin shall conceive, and bear a son, and shall call his name Immanuel" "which being interpreted is, God with us" (Isaiah 7:14; Matthew 1:23). He is the unique Son of God who came to save His people from their sins and to establish His throne of righteousness for eternity. Jesus' great aim in coming to this earth was to restore broken humanity and to reunite us with God in bonds of loving, unbreakable union. The Word was made flesh and dwelt among us, full of grace and truth, so that we might receive of His fullness and become children of grace among whom God would have His eternal habitation in the earth made new (see John 1:13, 14-16; Revelation 21:3, 4; and *The Desire of Ages*, pages 19-26).

Jesus' lowly birth was in keeping with the whole tenor of His mission; He came to save all, including the weakest, most broken, despised, and rejected people (see Luke 2:8-19; Isaiah 57:15; 61:1-3; 66:2). Though He was born in a barn, angels heralded His birth, for He was heaven's King descending on a royal mission to glorify God and reveal the way of peace. "Jesus purposed that no attraction of an earthly nature should call men to His side. Only the beauty of heavenly truth must draw those who would follow Him. The character of the Messiah had long been foretold in prophecy, and He desired men to accept Him upon the testimony of the word of God."[3]

A Rich Scriptural Passage

One of the richest Scripture passages highlighting the union of

Jesus' humanity and divinity is Philippians 2:5-8. Quite characteristically, this passage states the reality of that union without attempting to define how it was achieved. It does, however, clearly say that Jesus, though fully equal with the Father, divested Himself of His intrinsic divine powers and took upon Himself the form of a servant, humbling Himself to the obedience of death by crucifixion.

Jesus asserted that He did nothing apart from His Father's enabling will (see John 5:30; 7:16, 17; 8:28, 29, 42). He didn't rely on His inherent divinity to overcome temptation, to work miracles, or even to speak timely words of truth. Rather, He made Himself a surrendered vessel for the Father to do these works in and through Him. Thus He truly is our Representative, for as God's children, we have no power of our own to overcome sin or do the works of God. We can reach these goals only by the direct presence and action of God when we have surrendered our lives to Him (see Philippians 2:12, 13; Hebrews 1:1-3; 2:9-14; 1 John 3:5-9).

As the Second Adam, Jesus gained the victory where our first parents failed and where all have failed since. He has made it possible for us to become partakers of the divine nature and to live victorious over all sin and temptation through faith in His atoning blood.

"Wondrous combination of man and God! He might have helped his human nature to withstand the inroads of disease by pouring from his divine nature vitality and undecaying vigor to the human. But he humbled himself to man's nature. He did this that the Scripture might be fulfilled; and the plan was entered into by the Son of God, knowing all the steps in his humiliation, that he must descend to make an expiation for the sins of a condemned, groaning world. What humility was this! It amazed angels. The tongue can never describe it; the imagination can not take it in. The eternal Word consented to be made flesh! God became man! It was a wonderful humility."[4]

Read pages 49 and 117 in Ellen G. White's *The Desire of Ages,* considering as you do the enormous disadvantages under which Jesus labored in comparison to Adam prior to his fall. The question to be settled is not, "What advantages did Jesus possess that I am not naturally endowed with?" Rather, it is, "What advantages did Jesus come to *give us* through His incarnation, victorious life, and redeeming sacrifice?" He emptied Himself in His incarnation to fill us with the fullness of divine life in our regeneration.

In combating temptation on our behalf, Jesus relied on prayer and the Word of God, giving us an example by this practice (see Matthew 4:1-11; Hebrews 5:7-9). He made Himself subject to the Father for power to overcome. By making ourselves subject to Jesus and His Word, we may likewise overcome (see John 5:19, 20; 8:28). Unaided human nature in its fallen state cannot resist the devil. However, by the grace of Jesus mediated to us through His sacrifice, we can all become more than conquerors in the warfare against the assailing powers of evil (see Romans 8:1, 2, 31-39; Ephesians 6:10-18). Were Jesus' power not accessible to us, Satan would have free rein over our fallen nature. But to all who have faith in the efficacy of His blood, Jesus imparts all the strength they need for life's battle.

"As one of us [Jesus] was to give an example of obedience. For this He took upon Himself our nature, and passed through our experiences. 'In all things it behooved Him to be made like unto His brethren.' Heb. 2:17. If we had to bear anything which Jesus did not endure, then upon this point Satan would represent the power of God as insufficient for us. Therefore Jesus was 'in all points tempted like as we are.' Heb. 4:15. He endured every trial to which we are subject. And He exercised in His own behalf no power that is not freely offered to us. As man, He met temptation, and overcame in the strength given Him from God. He says, 'I delight to do Thy will, O My God: yea, Thy law is within My heart.' Ps. 40:8. As He went about doing good, and healing all who were afflicted by Satan, He made plain to men the character of God's law and the nature of His service. His life testifies that it is possible for us also to obey the law of God."[5]

Scripture gives clear evidence that Jesus developed as a human being by the same means that, under God's blessing, foster all human maturation of mind and body (see Luke 2:40, 51, 52; Philippians 2:6-8; see also *The Desire of Ages*, pages 70-74). "God sent forth his Son, made of a woman, made under the law" (Galatians 4:4). Through prayer, Scripture study, communion with God, and the cultivation of a spirit of obedience, Jesus developed beauty of character. He credits to His believing children all the victories He has achieved, and empowers us to live victoriously in His strength (see 1 Corinthians 10:13; Philippians 4:13).

Determined to negate the plan of salvation, Satan besieged Jesus from His birth till His crucifixion in an effort to make Him sin or to simply abandon His mission. So, Jesus was on the road to Calvary not just at the end of His earthly sojourn but throughout its course. "[Christ's] suffering did not begin or end with His manifestation in humanity. The cross is a revelation to our dull senses of that pain that, from its very inception, sin has brought to the heart of God."[6]

Tried Beyond Us

Those who worry that Jesus had some advantage that they are not naturally endowed with should consider that

- He experienced a level of suffering and temptation that no mortal has ever endured, or ever shall (see Lamentations 1:12; Mark 14:27-42; Luke 22:44);
- everything He did was for our benefit (see John 13:1-4);
- He died the second death in our place so that we would never have to undergo it, but instead have the joys of eternal life (see Luke 22:15, 16, 44; 1 Peter 3:18);
- and He has the knowledge, power, authority, grace, and willingness to deliver us from sin and make us partakers of His divine nature (see Isaiah 53:10-12; 2 Peter 1:4).

"The forgiveness of sins is not the sole result of the death of Jesus. He made the infinite sacrifice, not only that sin might be removed, but that human nature might be restored, rebeautified, reconstructed from its ruins, and made fit for the presence of God."[7] It is God's loving purpose to reproduce the character of His Son in every believer (see 2 Corinthians 3:17, 18). This is not a process of refined simulation, but of genuine assimilation, all attained through the blood of the everlasting covenant, not by any works of righteousness we may achieve or heights of moral aspiration we may reach (see Titus 3:5-7; Hebrews 13:20, 21).

Instead of worrying about our salvation and acceptance with God, we would do far better to contemplate joyously the mysteries and marvels of redemption and to let inspired praise lift our faith to new heights, greater freedom, and fullness of joy (see, e.g., Psalms 32; 51; 64; 103). Caught up in a tide of ecstasy over the magnificence of the gospel, Paul concluded his grand treatise to the Romans with this declamation: "To Him who is able to make you strong, according to the gospel I preach, and the proclamation concerning Jesus Christ, in harmony with the unveiling of the mystery shrouded in silence in ages past, but now brought to light, and by the command of the eternal God made known through the writings of the Prophets among all the Gentiles to win them to obedience to the faith—to God, the only wise, through Jesus Christ, even to Him be the glory through all the ages!" (Romans 16:25, 26, Weymouth).

If we let the rich reality of this experience enter our hearts, then the subject of the incarnation of Christ will no longer be to us merely a disputed dogma. Instead, it will bring forth a sustained doxology that will give our soul wings to fly away from our naturally sinful state and to enter eternal rest in Him, our Strength and Redeemer.

---

1. "Avoid every question in relation to the humanity of Christ which is liable to be misunderstood. Truth lies close to the track of presumption. In treating upon the humanity of Christ, you need to guard strenuously every assertion, lest your words be taken to mean more than they imply, and thus you lose or dim the clear perceptions of His humanity as combined with divinity. His birth was a miracle of God. . . .

"Never, in any way, leave the slightest impression upon human minds that a taint of, or inclination to, corruption rested upon Christ, or that He in any way yielded to corruption. He was tempted in all points like as man is tempted, yet He is called 'that holy thing.' It is a mystery that is left unexplained to mortals that Christ could be tempted in all points like as we are, and yet be without sin. The incarnation of Christ has ever been, and will ever remain a mystery. That which is revealed, is for us and for our children, but let every human being be warned from the ground of making Christ altogether human, such an one as ourselves; for it cannot be" (Ellen G. White, *Seventh-day Adventist Bible Commentary,* Francis D. Nichol, ed. (Hagerstown, Md.: Review and Herald, 1980), 5:1128, 1129.

One of the best compilations on this subject is Robert Olson's *The Humanity of Christ: Selections From the Writings of Ellen G. White* (Nampa, Idaho: Pacific Press®, 1989).

2. Ellen G. White, *The Upward Look* (Hagerstown, Md.: Review and Herald, 1982), 260.

3. Ellen G. White, *The Desire of Ages* (Nampa, Idaho: Pacific Press®, 1940), 43.

4. Ellen G. White, "Christ Man's Example," *Review & Herald,* September 4, 1900, 562.

5. White, *The Desire of Ages,* 24.

6. Ellen G. White, *Education* (Nampa, Idaho: Pacific Press®, 1952), 263. See also Isaiah 63:9; and *The Desire of Ages,* 114-131.

7. Ellen G. White, *Testimonies for the Church* (Nampa, Idaho: Pacific Press®, 1948), 5:537. See also John 1:12; 17:20-26; Ephesians 3:8-12, 16-19; 4:13-16; Romans 8:29.

CHAPTER 5

Days of Ministry in the Shadow of Calvary

"John saw Jesus coming toward him, and said, 'Behold! The Lamb of God who takes away the sin of the world!' " (John 1:29, NKJV). Though not recognizing the full significance of his words, John spoke them at the Spirit's prompting. He longed for the transforming touch of the Person who approached him on the banks of Jordan. Surely this was the King of glory! How amazing that He would ask for baptism at John's unworthy hands! Without a trace of pretended astonishment or false humility, John declared, "I need to be baptized by You!"

However, Jesus, as our Substitute and vicarious Sacrifice, came to take the steps repentant sinners must follow to become citizens of the heavenly kingdom (see Matthew 3:13-17). At His gentle but firm insistence, John administered the rite that inaugurated Him into His official calling as the Messiah, a calling that would penetrate the remotest depths of human need and ascend heroically to the summit of sacrifice on Calvary. By His daily deeds, Jesus caused justice to roll down like waters and righteousness like a mighty stream. Thus He turned the deserts of human lives into gardens of grace interwoven with streams of living water.

As Jesus emerged from the baptismal waters that signified His own death, burial, and resurrection, the Father proclaimed, "This is my beloved Son, in whom I am well pleased" (Matthew 3:17). On two other occasions in Jesus' ministry the Father repeated this affirmation, each time in reference to His Son's tryst with travail at Calvary and the glorious outcome of that mysterious rendezvous with death (see Matthew 17:5; John 12:27-33). Into a three-and-a-half-year ministry of service, Jesus crowded deeds of love, teachings of truth, and revelations of grace etched with immortal beauty. No day in His life was barren or idle. No day was sordid or frivolous. No day was moody or bitter. No day was prayerless or scattered. No day was squandered in self-pleasing, vain dreaming, or timid evasion. In His life was heaven never eclipsed, truth never muffled, love never clouded, mercy never lacking. Rejecting none, He drew the wayward and careworn to Himself with cords of love. All the concerted forces of darkness couldn't obstruct the blessings He came to bring, nor alter Heaven's resolve to make Calvary the thoroughfare to salvation for everyone seeking deliverance.

Though infinitely joyous, Jesus was also a Man of sorrows and acquainted with grief—a paradox resolved by the revealed mysteries of divine love applied to our salvation. "As one with us, [Christ] must bear the burden of our guilt and woe. The Sinless One must feel the shame of sin. The peace lover must dwell with strife, the truth must abide with falsehood, purity with vileness. Every sin, every discord, every defiling lust that transgression had brought, was torture to His spirit. . . .

"Upon Him who had laid off His glory and accepted the weakness of humanity the redemption of the world must rest. He saw and felt it all, but His purpose remained steadfast. Upon His arm depended the salvation of the fallen race, and He reached out His hand to grasp the hand of Omnipotent Love."[1]

Nothing could distract Jesus from His aim to seek and save the lost. Knowing that His work on earth would culminate on Calvary, He steadily moved toward that goal, flinching not and without either morbid feelings or reckless abandon, sustained by His Father's love and grace and His own longing for our redemption.

A Promised Forerunner

Through Malachi, God promised that He would send a forerunner who would prepare people's hearts to receive the Messiah. This individual would call people to deep repentance. John the Baptist fulfilled the prophecy. He emphasized that we must treat all, friend and foe alike, as brothers. He summarized the moral message of Scripture, the golden rule and brotherly covenant applied (see Matthew 7:13). But he did far more too. Only one power—Jesus revealed and received—can uproot human corruption and prejudice. John made it clear that repentance and remission of sins are divine gifts mediated to us through the Lamb. He made no allowance for even the parenthetic inclusion of meritorious works in the formula of redemption. Such passages as Matthew 3:2, 6-12; 4:17; 7:13-23; and John 3:11-21, 27-35 show that John's words faithfully mirrored those of Jesus and emphasized the need to receive Jesus' testimony in full, without reservation.

High authorities, enraged by John's fidelity to God's Word and will, beheaded him. Jesus linked John's martyrdom with His own impending sacrifice (see Mark 6:14-31; Matthew 7:10-14). He identified John as the prophesied Elijah of Malachi 4:5, 6 (see Matthew 17:11; cp. Luke 1:17).

John's life, replete with lessons for the heralds of Jesus' second coming, was characterized by Spirit-filled self-abnegation. This fruit of his fervent love for Jesus was the secret of his towering spiritual strength and influence. Our walk and witness are to be similar to his, especially with regard to magnifying the centrality of Jesus' atoning sacrifice. The call to behold the Lamb of God is no static invitation. His manifold grace and glory supply an eternity's worth of intimate revelations for our study. To behold the Lamb in the fullness of His glory is to become saturated with the power and magnificence of the gospel. It is to have satisfying fellowship with Jesus, in whose presence life is transformed and eternal joys abound. It is to see the purposes of God illuminated. It is to possess the key to every moral and intellectual question that cries out for an answer. (See Revelation 5:1-14; 7:13-17; 14:1; 15:2-4.)

"The sacrifice of Christ as an atonement for sin is the great truth around which all other truths cluster. In order to be rightly understood and appreciated, every truth in the Word of God, from Genesis to Revelation, must be studied in the light which streams from the cross of Calvary, and in connection with the wondrous, central truth of the Saviour's atonement. Those who study the Redeemer's wonderful sacrifice grow in grace and knowledge."[2]

Jesus' work on earth was not to dazzle people with His splendor and authority but to seek and save the lost. Divine love incarnate, He healed the sick of every affliction and released multitudes from Satan's bondage. Truth came from Jesus' lips not as an untested theory, but as a living power that He fully exemplified. For this reason "there followed him great multitudes of people from Galilee" and regions beyond (Matthew 4:25).

"He came to this world as the unwearied servant of man's necessity. Love for the lost race was manifested in all that He said and did. He clothed His divinity with humanity, that He might stand among human beings as one of them, a sharer of their poverty and their griefs. . . . Day by day He might be seen entering the humble abodes of want and sorrow, speaking hope to the downcast and peace to the distressed. . . . Humble, gracious, tenderhearted, pitiful, He went about doing good, lifting up the bowed-down and comforting the sorrowful. None who came to Him went away unhelped. To all He brought hope and gladness. Wherever He went He carried blessing."[3]

Since His ministry was one of love—pure in motive, uplifting in its steady flow—why did the religious leaders and eventually the majority of people reject Jesus with such fierce hatred? It is because sinful human nature is under the control of Satan; it is hostile to God and loves darkness rather than light. It will not tolerate the clear, unblemished manifestation of truth (see John 3:19-21; 15:17-25; Romans 8:7).

Those who are born after the flesh persecute those who are born after the Spirit; the carnal nature is implacably at odds with the character and will of God (see Galatians 4:29; Ephesians 4:17-19). People who regarded themselves as righteous in their own merits felt condemned by His life of purity and benevolence, which they did not seek or desire. To admit their need for a new heart would have challenged their pride. They regarded the call to repentance as an affront to their dignity, an implied accusation that they were not sufficiently spiritual. Like Cain, determined to silence the voice of entreaty and reproof, they rejected the compassionate but unflattering appeal of the gospel and let murderous resentment toward Jesus twine about their hearts (see Romans 2:4-8; 1 Thessalonians 2:15, 16). Today, as then, Satan strives to blind people to the beauty and imperative necessity of the gospel (see 2 Corinthians 4:3, 4).

Despite all the forms of opposition arrayed against Him, Jesus did not fail nor become discouraged. He had His Father's approval and support. All who desired salvation from sin welcomed His words. They exercised the integrity and moral courage to reject all that was false and evil, both without and within. Truth is supremely beautiful and appealing, but it offers no solace to corruption of heart, no complicity with self-deception. Jesus said, "Blessed is he who is not offended because of Me" (Matthew 11:6, NKJV). Let that be our resolve.

A Baptism of Blood

Toward the close of His work on earth, Jesus referred with increasing frequency to the baptism of blood awaiting Him at Jerusalem. He wished to anchor His disciples in the meaning of His sacrifice. He especially wanted them to understand that His crucifixion signaled not the defeat, but the triumph, of His mission.

But the disciples did not welcome the revelation that the thorn must come before the throne, the cross before the crown. So preoccupied were they with the question of who was the greatest among them that any mention of Jesus' impending sacrifice shook their dreams of worldly fame and favor. At this stage their "heart was hardened" (Mark 6:52; 8:17). In their spiritual dimness they found Jesus' mention of the cross baffling and repugnant. Was not self-sacrificing love meant to be used as a rare spice for grand occasions rather than as life's principal ingredient?

Jesus' apparent lack of acumen, His impractical idealism as He repeatedly turned aside from opportunities to seize the reins of political power, offended them. "He was in the world, and the world was made by him, and the world knew him not. He came unto his own, and his own received him not" (John 1:10, 11). Truly, Jesus trod the winepress of sacrifice alone, and of the people none was with Him (see Isaiah 63:3).

Yet the disciples were sincere. They had much to learn and very much to unlearn, as we all do. As the time of Calvary drew near, Peter acknowledged Jesus' Messiahship with ringing assurance (see Matthew 16:13-20). Jesus commended him for that recognition and affirmed that His Father had revealed this truth to him. But moments later, the glory of this scene was shattered. Peter rebuked his Master for affirming His resolve to go to Jerusalem to die at the hands of wicked men. Jesus quickly showed him the error of this protest. "Peter did not desire to see the cross in the work of Christ. The impression which his words would make was directly opposed to that which Christ desired to make on the minds of His followers, and the Saviour was moved to utter one of the sternest rebukes that ever fell from His lips: 'Get thee behind Me, Satan: thou art an offense unto Me: for thou savorest not the things that be of God, but those that be of men.' "[4]

But amid the falling shadows, radiant glory was to shine forth for the disciples. With Peter, James, and John, Jesus withdrew for prayer to a high mountain (see Matthew 17:1-9). There He sought strength from His Father to consummate His mission. Further, He knew that His disciples were altogether unprepared for the crisis. Burdened with the mounting opposition of the religious leaders, with the memory of John the Baptist's recent beheading, and with Jesus' warning of His imminent trials, a sense of foreboding settled upon the disciples.

"The Saviour has seen the gloom of His disciples, and has longed to lighten their grief by an assurance that their faith has not been in vain. . . . Now the burden of His prayer is that they may be given a manifestation of the glory He had with the Father before the world was, that His kingdom may be revealed to human eyes, and that His disciples may be strengthened to behold it. He pleads that they may witness a manifestation of His divinity that will comfort them in the hour of His supreme agony with the knowledge that He is of a surety the Son of God and that His shameful death is a part of the plan of redemption.

"His prayer is heard. While He is bowed in lowliness upon the stony ground, suddenly the heavens open . . . and holy radiance descends upon the mount, enshrouding the Saviour's form. Divinity from within flashes through humanity, and meets the glory coming from above. Arising from His prostrate position, Christ stands in godlike majesty. The soul agony is gone. His countenance now shines 'as the sun,' and His garments are 'white as the light.' "[5]

Moses and Elijah appeared and spoke with Jesus "of his decease [*exodos*, in Greek] which he should accomplish at Jerusalem" (Luke 9:30, 31). They recognized the epic significance of Calvary and saw Jesus' death as love's crowning conquest rather than its crushing defeat.

After the supernatural light faded and Moses and Elijah disappeared, Peter expressed his uncomprehending awe by making the grandiose suggestion that they build three shrines there—one each for Jesus, Moses, and Elijah. This event was not, however, to be hallowed with lifeless structures but with the enshrining of Jesus' instruction in their hearts and their undeviating obedience to it. This lesson stands forever.

Last Journey to Jerusalem

As Jesus led His disciples on their last journey together to Jerusalem, He told them plainly that "all things that are written by the prophets concerning the Son of man shall be accomplished" there; for "the Son of man shall be betrayed unto the chief priests and unto the scribes, and they shall condemn Him to death, and shall deliver him to the Gentiles to mock, and to scourge, and to crucify him: and the third day he shall rise again" (Luke 18:31; Matthew 20:18, 19).

This revelation of impending events should have turned the disciples' interest to the teachings of the prophets concerning these matters. But "they understood none of these things: . . . neither knew they the things which were spoken" (Luke 18:34). Once again this was not because Jesus' words were unclear or enigmatic, but because His purposes were so foreign to the disciples' aims and expectations. Jesus had, after all, commissioned them to proclaim everywhere that "the kingdom of heaven is at hand," and promised that they would be enthroned as judges of Israel (see Matthew 19:27-30). Stimulated by this promise, James and John, through Salome, their mother, asked Jesus for the places of highest honor in His kingdom (see Matthew 20:20-28; Mark 10:35-45). Stung because they hadn't made this request for themselves first, the other disciples resented James and John for their enterprising audacity.

James and John's request smacked heavily of egotism, yet Jesus didn't rebuke them or their mother for coveting honors so incongruous with His character and mission. Instead, He sought to deepen and purify their love for Him and their attachment to His cause. He pointed them to the cup He was to drink and the baptism with which He was to be baptized. Vaguely they sensed His meaning as they asserted their readiness to share His sufferings. Numerous lessons awaited them on the path of true discipleship, but ultimately they both found strength—James to endure martyrdom, and John to endure a life of labor and persecution. They entered into ennobling fellowship with Jesus' sufferings (see Mark 10:38, 39; 14:32-36; Luke 12:50; cp. Acts 12:2; Revelation 1:9; Philippians 3:10).

"The one who stands nearest to Christ will be he who on earth has drunk most deeply of the spirit of His self-sacrificing love,—love that 'vaunteth not itself, is not puffed up, . . . seeketh not her own, is not easily provoked, thinketh no evil' (1 Cor. 13:4, 5),—love that moves the disciple, as it moved our Lord, to give all, to live and labor and sacrifice, even unto death, for the saving of humanity."[6]

Of all Jesus' disciples, Mary Magdalene had the deepest grasp of His appointment at Calvary. She knew that such love as His would not escape the enmity of the self-righteous, and that such forgiveness as His was purchased at a cost that outweighed the whole world's false glory and real disgrace. She expressed her loyal-hearted love in outpoured spikenard and kisses and tears for which she owed no apology. The wordless eloquence of her act reverberates in memory long after all boastful vows have ceased to echo. If today we had more of Mary's self-abandoning dedication to Jesus, the aroma of the gospel would pervade the world like tabernacle incense mingled with the myrrh of Paradise.

---

1. Ellen G. White, *The Desire of Ages* (Nampa, Idaho: Pacific Press®, 1940), 111.

2. Ellen G. White, *Sons and Daughters of God* (Hagerstown, Md.: Review and Herald, 1983), 221.

3. Ellen G. White, *Testimonies for the Church* (Nampa, Idaho: Pacific Press®, 1948), 7:221.

4. White, *The Desire of Ages*, 415, 416.

5. Ibid., 420, 421.

6. Ibid., 549.

The Crimson Trail

It is Jesus' golden moment of triumph. Admirers flock to hail Him as Israel's King. Mounted on a donkey, He follows the Bethany road's winding course toward Jerusalem while the crowd increases in numbers and rapturous enthusiasm, waving palm branches and shouting accolades. Rounding a bend, the procession comes to a spacious overlook. Jesus stops there and gazes at the city below, His eyes resting on the temple, resplendent in the western sun. The entire crowd looks at His face to discern marks of admiration and joy. Instead, they see Jesus' "eyes fill with tears, and His body rock to and fro like a tree before the tempest, while a wail of anguish bursts from His quivering lips, as if from the depths of a broken heart. . . .

"The tears of Jesus were not in anticipation of His own suffering. . . . His was no selfish sorrow. The thought of His own agony did not intimidate that noble, self-sacrificing soul. It was the sight of Jerusalem that pierced the heart of Jesus—Jerusalem that had rejected the Son of God and scorned His love, that refused to be convinced by His mighty miracles, and was about to take His life. He saw what she was in her guilt of rejecting her Redeemer, and what she might have been had she accepted Him who alone could heal her wound. He had come to save her; how could He give her up?"[1]

Jesus' final week before Calvary is a tapestry of events that illuminate His mission, which was destined to climax in supreme suffering and glory. In this final Passover week, amid the gathering storm, Jesus demonstrated the valor of self-sacrificing love on a more than epic scale. His words and actions personify truths that stand as an unassailable city of refuge for all who flee to Him for salvation.

Through the use of a Bible dictionary or similar helps, one can find a chronological outline of the events in Jesus' earthly life. One discovers that about a third of the material in the four Gospels deals explicitly with the week leading up to Jesus' crucifixion and resurrection. A synoptic reading of the Gospels yields an integrated picture of these events.

It's helpful to have a brief outline of the period often termed the "Passion Week"—from the Sunday or Monday prior to Jesus' crucifixion to the following Sunday, when He rose from the grave. God's statutes ordered that the Passover lamb be slain on the evening of the fourteenth day of the first month (originally called *Abib* in Hebrew, and later, *Nisan*), which came in the early spring (see Exodus 12:1-6; 34:18; Esther 3:7).

Reckoning the days from midnight to midnight for conveniently chronicling the flow of events, the high points of the week may be outlined as follows:

Sunday (Nisan 9): The triumphal entry, Jesus' silent visit to the temple, and return to Bethany, 1.5 miles (2.5 km.) east of Jerusalem.

Monday (Nisan 10): The cursing of the fruitless fig tree and the second cleansing of the temple. Jesus heals the afflicted there and returns to Bethany in the evening.

Tuesday (Nisan 11): Jesus' last day in the temple; the Greek believers meet with Jesus in the outer court. His last day of public teaching, woes against religious elite, retirement to the Mount of Olives, and Jesus' discourse there on the Second Coming. Judas clinches the betrayal with the priests that night.

Wednesday (Nisan 12): Jesus in quiet retirement with His disciples.

Thursday (Nisan 13): Preparation for the Passover, the Lord's Supper, Judas's betrayal, Jesus' farewell discourse and high-priestly prayer for the disciples, Gethsemane, and the arrest in the Garden. (Thursday night, when the events that followed the Lord's Supper occurred, was the fourteenth of Nisan by Jewish reckoning.)

Friday (Nisan 14): Jesus led to Annas, then to Caiaphas, then to the Sanhedrin. Peter's denial; Jesus brought to Pilate, then to Herod's palace, where He is mocked and abused, and then back to Pilate, who strives in vain to release Him. He is scourged, condemned, and led away to be crucified.

During this momentous week, so resonant with portents of Calvary, Jesus' chief concern was to strengthen His disciples to meet the crisis with informed faith. He wanted them to know that the ravages awaiting Him were not the overthrow of His mission but its triumph, and that His travail would not wound His love for them and all humanity, but rather heal sin's fatal wounds (see John 13:1; 15:7-20).

Time for All to Know

In His triumphal procession through Jerusalem, Jesus willingly accepts homage because the time had come for all to know that He was truly the Messiah and the ultimate Passover Lamb (see Mark 11:7-11; Luke 19:29-40; Matthew 21:1-11). "It was His purpose . . . to call attention to the sacrifice that was to crown His mission to a fallen world. While the people were assembling at Jerusalem to celebrate the Passover, He, the antitypical Lamb, by a voluntary act set Himself apart as an oblation. It would be needful for His church in all succeeding ages to make His death for the sins of the world a subject of deep thought and study. Every fact connected with it should be verified beyond a doubt. It was necessary, then, that the eyes of all people should now be directed to Him; the events which preceded His great sacrifice must be such as to call attention to the sacrifice itself. After such a demonstration as that attending His entry into Jerusalem, all eyes would follow His rapid progress to the final scene."[2]

In the swelling crowd gathered around Jesus were many whom He had healed and set free from the darkness of demon-possession during the past several years. Knowing this, the religious leaders burned with envy, malice, and rage. "Compel this vulgar rabble to cease their acclamations," they demanded of Him. But He calmly replied, "I tell you that, if these should hold their peace, the stones would immediately cry out." Entering Jerusalem, Jesus quietly surveyed the temple with its unholy traffic. Then, unnoticed, He withdrew to Bethany.

On the next day Jesus returned to the temple and cast out the moneychangers, while openly condemning the whole system of priestcraft that had dislodged true worship and turned Judaism into a complete travesty of the gospel truths taught by the prophets of old. Jesus' action cleared the way for the outcast and disabled to come to Him for healing and salvation, the very functions for which God intended the temple and its services to stand with richly inviting effect (see Mark 11:11-19; Matthew 21:12-16, Isaiah 56:4-8; Jeremiah 7:8-15).

How brutally ironic that the animals that symbolized Jesus' sacrifice were being sold by the priests for exorbitant profits! Thus were trampled underfoot the glorious gospel lessons embodied in the sanctuary services. Grieved by this outrage, Jesus exerted His authority to cleanse His Father's temple of the unholy traffic that had made His house of prayer a den of thieves. This action cleared the way for the afflicted to press about Him and receive His salvation and healing "without money and without price."

The next day, Tuesday of the Passion Week, was Jesus' last day of public teaching. As He and the apostles descended the Mount of Olives for His final visit to the temple, they saw the fig tree that Jesus had cursed. Its withered state signified the sentence of condemnation Israel had incurred for its willful rejection of Him as the Messiah (see John 15:22-25).

Learning that Jesus had returned to the temple and taught the people, the chief priests bustled forward and demanded that He tell them on what authority He acted. By evading His question regarding John the Baptist's authority, they exposed their treacherous duplicity. Jesus told them three parables in quick succession designed to warn them of the dire consequences of their evil plot (see Matthew 21:20-22:15). He modeled a love for His enemies that was too pure to excuse sin and too deep to withhold a final appeal. Poignant beyond comparison is His lament for wayward, rebellious Jerusalem (see Matthew 23:37-39).

In the course of that last day at the temple, Greek converts to Judaism came to the outer court to seek Jesus. He took this opportunity to speak of His sacrifice so soon to take place and its resulting harvest of glory (see John 12:20-33). "I, if I be lifted up from the earth, will draw all men unto Me," He said. Ellen G. White wrote that He was saying, "If I become the propitiation for the sins of men, the world will be lighted up. Satan's hold upon the souls of men will be broken. The defaced image of God will be restored in humanity, and a family of believing saints will finally inherit the heavenly home. This is the result of Christ's death. The Saviour is lost in contemplation of the scene of triumph called up before Him. He sees the cross, the cruel, ignominious cross, with all its attending horrors, blazing with glory.

"But the work of human redemption is not all that is accomplished by the cross. The love of God is manifested to the universe. The prince of this world is cast out. The accusations which Satan has brought against God are refuted. The reproach which he has cast upon heaven is forever removed."[3]

After leaving the temple as the day waned, Jesus and His disciples ascended the Mount of Olives overlooking Jerusalem. Here He carefully outlined the events that would lead up to His second coming and gave three parables on the judgment—thus emphasizing the ultimate outcome of His sacrifice and the universal authority of His kingdom that was sure to triumph over the forces of evil now marshaling against Him, forces that would relentlessly continue pushing for supremacy until the close of time (see Matthew 24; 25; Mark 13; Luke 21).

After a day's interlude for quiet reflection with Jesus, the disciples made preparations for the Passover. Fully aware that He was the true Paschal Lamb who was to be sacrificed, Jesus wished to spend His few remaining peaceful hours with His disciples for their comfort and instruction. How moving are His words: "With desire I have desired to eat this passover with you before I suffer" (Luke 22:15).

At this time the disciples' chief concern was, "Who is the greatest among us?" Misbegotten pride froze their spirituality and blinded them to the solemn magnificence of what was happening before them. Each was playing the petty bureaucrat, while they should all have been gathering lessons in the sovereign glories of self-abnegating love. To help melt this darkness of self-exaltation, Jesus washed the disciples' feet at the Passover supper (see Luke 22:24-34; John 13:1-25).

Inexhaustible are the lessons connected with the Lord's Supper regarding the substance and power of the new covenant, the qualities of true discipleship, and the indomitable vitality of the Cross to achieve the full triumph of heaven's purposes as stated in Ephesians 1:3-23 and Colossians 1:9-23. The Communion service diagrams the gospel in brief, with Jesus as the dispenser of all its life-transforming power and blessings. Let us awaken to its glory, forget personal advantage, renounce rivalry, and submerge ourselves in Jesus!

The Divine Medium of Communication

On this last evening with His disciples, Jesus spoke extensively of the Holy Spirit's work, because the Spirit would be His representative, the divine medium for the communication of every benefit ensuing from His sacrifice (see John 14:16-18, 25-27; 15:26, 27; 16:12-15). The elements of Jesus' last will and testament in such places as John 14:1-3, 19-24; 15:7-17; and 16:22-24, 33 still bless those who contemplate them.

"In describing to His disciples the office work of the Holy Spirit, Jesus sought to inspire them with the joy and hope that inspired His own heart. He rejoiced because of the abundant help He had provided for His church. The Holy Spirit was the highest of all gifts that He could solicit from His Father for the exaltation of His people. The Spirit was to be given as a regenerating agent, and without this the sacrifice of Christ would have been of no avail. . . . It is the Spirit that makes effectual what has been wrought out by the world's Redeemer. . . . Christ has given His Spirit as a divine power to overcome all hereditary and cultivated tendencies to evil, and to impress His own character upon His church."[4]

Just before His travail in Gethsemane, Jesus presented to His Father the request that His disciples in all ages would enter into spiritual oneness with Himself and be filled with the same love that flourishes between the Father and the Son. His prayer that all His redeemed would have the privilege of dwelling with Him forever reveals the infinitely glorious aims of His sacrifice. This petition should be the guiding light for our spiritual lives, for it sets forth with concentrated clarity the fullness of God's glorious purpose for us. What folly it would be to allow anything to interfere with the fulfillment of Jesus' intercessory prayer on our behalf!

Jesus entered Gethsemane with His three most intimate disciples and told them to pray and watch lest they enter temptation. Three times He prayed to His Father for release from the excruciating horror of the cross if any other way could be found for the salvation of humanity. But submission to His Father's will was the paramount principle that held Him on course to Calvary (see Matthew 26:36-44; Mark 14:32-42; Luke 22:39-44; Revelation 14:10).

Even while Jesus was pleading for strength to save lost and guilty man, a maelstrom of treason and treachery against Him was gathering momentum. As Satan plied all his arts to discourage Jesus, Judas was leading a band of religious mobsters to arrest Him.

Jesus' heart was so deeply pierced with supernatural grief that He was already shedding His blood for the sins of humanity—even before the spikes of Golgotha bit into His flesh. He drank the gall of our guilt and shame that He might give us the nectar of His innocence and mercy. For us He drained the cup of wrath, to offer in its place the cup of reconciliation. His appointed exchange of roles to become sin for us made His suffering in Gethsemane almost unendurable (see 2 Corinthians 5:21; Isaiah 53:10). It was all for the sake of our becoming the righteousness of God in Him. This knowledge braced Him to pay the high cost of our salvation. Unless we understand the heinousness of sin and God's judicial wrath against it, the vicarious sufferings that Jesus bore on our behalf are an impenetrable enigma.

"As the Son of God bowed in the attitude of prayer in the Garden of Gethsemane, the agony of His spirit forced from His pores sweat like great drops of blood. It was here that the horror of great darkness surrounded Him. The sins of the world were upon Him. He was suffering in man's stead as a transgressor of His Father's law. Here was the scene of temptation. The divine light of God was receding from His vision, and He was passing into the hands of the powers of darkness. In His soul anguish He lay prostrate on the cold earth. He was realizing His Father's frown. He had taken the cup of suffering from the lips of guilty man, and proposed to drink it Himself, and in its place give to man the cup of blessing. The wrath that would have fallen upon man was now falling upon Christ. It was here that the mysterious cup trembled in His hand. . . .

"It was a sense of His Father's frown, in consequence of sin, which rent His heart with such piercing agony and forced from His brow great drops of blood."[5]

God sent an angel to strengthen Jesus so that He could be our Sin Bearer. And it was all for love to us, love that will not compromise holy principle or cancel justice. Love poured out in measureless torrents of mercy for our redemption. Love that will not let us go unless we spurn it for the love of sin and turn the gold of opportunity into the dross of rejection.

1. Ellen G. White, *The Desire of Ages* (Nampa, Idaho: Pacific Press®, 1940), 575, 576.

2. Ibid., 571.

3. Ibid., 625, 626.

4. Ibid., 671.

5. Ellen G. White, *Testimonies for the Church* (Nampa, Idaho: Pacific Press®, 1948), 2:203, 204.

CHAPTER 7

Passage to Calvary

Alexander Whyte, a Scottish minister, awakened one night groaning in agony. Aroused from her sleep, his wife asked, "Alex, are you ill?" "Oh," he replied, "I've just had the most horrible dream. I seemed to be standing in the judgment hall, close to where Jesus was being scourged. I saw His form gashed with each fiery stroke. The soldier wielding the lash took evident delight in his task. Anger and indignation boiled up in me. I cried to the tormentor, 'Stop this cruelty at once. You are smiting the Lord.' As he raised the whip again, I seized his arm and—turning to face me with an icy leer—that soldier was me!"

Pastor Whyte graphically saw in his dream a truth hard for us all to face—that not only are we healed with the stripes of Jesus, but by our unchristlike ways, we have inflicted stripes on Him. In the events leading up to the Cross we see unveiled with soul-searching appeal a microcosm of human attitudes toward God. We also see a striking display of how miserably lost we are. Our condition is curable only through the sufferings Jesus bore in those desperate hours from Gethsemane to Golgotha. How we wish the cost of our redemption need not have been so high! But it was, and what an insult to God to reject salvation for any reason, whether from a feeling of unworthiness on our part or from a deluded sense that we don't need it.

Doubtless, we are all unworthy of Jesus' salvation and the price He paid to ransom us. But He paid a price that invests us with value beyond estimate. If anyone feels above the need for redemption, he knows neither God nor himself. God has not overestimated the magnitude of our sins, nor has He overestimated the price required to save us.

In the Garden of Gethsemane Jesus counted afresh the high cost of His impending travail. Braced by His Father's assurance that His sacrifice would prevail, no oncoming sorrow or pain could deter Him from His rendezvous with death, for in that encounter He would conquer death in its own domain and bring life and immortality to light.

While Jesus lingered in prayer, His disciples slept their sorrow-laden sleep. Then the flash of lanterns and the clatter of swords and clubs borne by the angry mob that burst into the Garden jolted them awake. Rising with a start, they prepared to defend themselves and their Lord.

As the rabble set upon Jesus with "haste to shed innocent blood" (Isaiah 59:7, cp. John 18:2-9), God mercifully gave them an opportunity to recognize their crime. "No traces of His recent agony were visible as Jesus stepped forth to meet His betrayer. Standing in advance of His disciples He said, 'Whom seek ye?' They answered, 'Jesus of Nazareth.' Jesus replied, 'I am He.' As these words were spoken, the angel who had lately ministered to Jesus moved between Him and the mob. A divine light illuminated the Saviour's face, and a dovelike form overshadowed Him. In the presence of this divine glory, the murderous throng could not stand for a moment. They staggered back. Priests, elders, soldiers, and even Judas, fell as dead men to the ground.

"The angel withdrew, and the light faded away. Jesus had opportunity to escape, but He remained, calm and self-possessed. As one glorified He stood in the midst of that hardened band, now prostrate and helpless at His feet. The disciples looked on, silent with wonder and awe."[1]

Jesus' answer, "I am . . . ," echoed the name by which He identified Himself to Moses in the wilderness (see Exodus 3:11-14; John

61

8:58; Revelation 22:13; 1 Corinthians 10:1-4). Jesus was not God's envoy, but God without alloy. His humanity was the vehicle dedicated to redeem lost human beings. But few prized the gift, and Satan was determined to trample salvation underfoot and sink it deep into the mire of rude unbelief.

Repressing conviction and rallying their brute courage, the improvised posse of priests, temple police, and hirelings sprang to their feet and surrounded Jesus. Without hesitation He identified Himself as the One they sought; Judas need not have planted his kiss of betrayal, but, as Satan's bondservant, he carried out his nefarious work. Although rabbinic law forbade the binding of a man before judicial condemnation, the mob tied Jesus tightly, intending to take Him directly to the high priest's palace. Suddenly Peter strode forward, and, swinging his sword at Malchus's head, he severed his right ear. With calm, irresistible authority, Jesus freed His hands to heal the wound, while rebuking the notion that carnal weapons may be used in defense of the gospel. Then, with perfect composure, He resumed His position as prisoner. He who loosed people from bondage and let the oppressed go free allowed His hands to be fettered and His freedom to be taken.

Seeing that Jesus wouldn't fight, the disciples ran away, offended and afraid. It seemed that the gates of hell had prevailed against the fledgling church at the crucial hour. Truly, the Shepherd was smitten, and the sheep were scattered. He trod the winepress alone, and of the people there was none with Him. Who can fathom Jesus' loneliness on this frenzied night that was steeped in the sulfurous tang of blood, sweat, and rage? He had come to conquer the wrathful dragon (see Revelation 12:9), and this was the death struggle. Jesus would employ only the regal weapons of righteousness and truth, but Satan would utilize the cruelest of devices, as he strove by insult and violence to goad the Redeemer into an ungodly reaction. This wickedness would not go unpunished, but that must come in a future setting of infinite dignity and perfect justice. Jesus' present mission, however, was to redeem the lost. To accomplish it, He must suffer infinite humiliation and abuse from the very creatures He came to save.

Now that Jesus was in their clutches, the Sanhedrin faced the thorny challenge of contriving charges against Him that would condemn Him to death under Roman law. But what accusations could they formulate? Jesus hadn't taught or done anything subversive. His every word and action, if rightly represented, would redound to His vindication, attest to His messiahship, and expose the vileness of His accusers. From here onward everything they did had to be a lie enacted against the embodiment of eternal Truth. Though presumably a court of justice guided by divine law, the Sanhedrin were bent on destroying the Lawgiver. They overrode the rabbinic principle that an accused person was innocent until proven guilty. Deep in their hearts they felt, "This is the heir: come, let us kill him, that the inheritance may be ours" (Luke 20:14). They must fabricate charges that would make Jesus appear to be a disturber of the peace and enemy of the state.

Though Jewish law forbade such proceedings at night, they led Jesus to the retired high priest, Annas, the wily father-in-law of Caiaphas, the current high priest. When Jesus reminded the haughty former high priest of his official duty to require credible witnesses against Him to substantiate any charges, a temple officer slapped His face. How Jesus must have been tempted to manifest His divine sovereignty to these cruel inquisitors as they violated every rule of justice against Him, the rightful Judge of all! But "His love for His Father, and His pledge, made from the foundation of the world, to become the Sin Bearer, led Him to endure uncomplainingly the coarse treatment of those He came to save. It was a part of His mission to bear, in His humanity, all the taunts and abuse that men could heap upon Him. The only hope of humanity was in this submission of Christ to all that He could endure from the hands and hearts of men."[2]

Unable to lure Jesus into incriminating Himself, Annas sent Him to a select session of the Sanhedrin, with Caiaphas presiding. They resorted to the expedient of hiring false witnesses against Him (see Matthew 26:59-62; Mark 14:55-60). Jesus listened with patience to the discordant, contradictory charges brought against Him by uncouth men whose words jangled with the clink of bribe money. What consolation this provides His children who have had to endure perjury and misrepresentation, knowing that those who hated Jesus for His innocence impeached Him, the Incarnation of truth and justice, with acrimonious lies!

Jesus' serene bearing and blameless record won the sympathies of those observing the rage of His judges, who by Jewish law should have been His defenders and protectors. Floundering to concoct a case, the Sanhedrin plowed on with their grim burlesque of justice. Finally, with desperate cunning, Caiaphas framed the fatal question, "I adjure Thee by the living God that Thou tell us whether Thou be the Christ, the Son of God." Knowing that His affirmative answer was His death warrant in their eyes, Jesus would not deny His identity or His relation to His Father. He warned the court, however, that someday they would see Him in His divine authority. Then they would remember with anguish this infamous night when they ripped justice to shreds and exulted in their malicious madness! (See Matthew 26:64; Revelation 1:7; see also *The Desire of Ages,* pp. 706–708.)

Shrieking with pretended horror over Jesus' alleged blasphemy, Caiaphas tore his robe. In Levitical law this sacrilegious deed warranted his own execution (see Leviticus 10:6; 21:10). But Caiaphas called for the sentence of death upon Jesus. As one man, the Sanhedrin bellowed their confirmation.

Once the Sanhedrin pronounced this sentence, a cyclone of violence burst upon Jesus. With satanic fury, priests and counselors derided and buffeted Him. They had Him detained until the morning, when, in full council, they could "legally" condemn Him to death and obtain the governor's sanction.

Having seen the cruelty with which He was treated before the council, the ignorant rabble "took license to manifest all the satanic elements of their nature. Christ's very nobility and godlike bearing goaded them to madness. His meekness, His innocence, His majestic patience, filled them with hatred born of Satan. Mercy and justice were trampled upon. Never was criminal treated in so inhuman a manner as was the Son of God.

"But a keener anguish rent the heart of Jesus; the blow that inflicted the deepest pain no enemy's hand could have dealt."[3] After fleeing from the Garden of Gethsemane, Peter and John rallied sufficient courage to follow Jesus to the high priest's palace. John, knowing the family of Annas, gained admittance for himself and Peter.

Peter joined the servants and soldiers around a fire in the courtyard and listened to the proceedings. Repeatedly identified as one of Jesus' followers, Peter denied knowing Him, just as Jesus had foretold. Peter clinched his repudiation with cursing and swearing to prove the impossibility of his association with such a man (see Mark 14:66-72; Luke 22:55-58; John 18:24-28). What an eternal warning against all spiritual self-confidence! If we are to confess Jesus in the hour of supreme trial, then we must heed His words of reproof and warning to us and not deflect them, as Peter did, thinking Jesus' judgment unfair (see Mark 14:27-34, 37, 38; Revelation 3:14-21).

Nowhere in the annals of human tragedy do we find a more poignant scene than the one recorded in Luke 22:59-62: Jesus' look at Peter at the crucial moment of his third denial. "While the degrading oaths were fresh upon Peter's lips, and the shrill crowing of the cock was still ringing in his ears, the Saviour turned from the frowning judges, and looked full upon His poor disciple. At the same time Peter's eyes were drawn to his Master. In that gentle countenance he read deep pity and sorrow, but there was no anger there.

"The sight of that pale, suffering face, those quivering lips, that look of compassion and forgiveness, pierced his heart. . . . Once more he looked at his Master, and saw a sacrilegious hand raised to smite Him in the face. Unable longer to endure the scene, he rushed, heartbroken, from the hall."[4]

In the morning the Sanhedrin—minus its members of good character, who had purposely not been notified of the meeting—convened to ratify their earlier sentence. After treating Jesus with even worse brutality than before (see *The Desire of Ages,* pages 714, 715), they shoved Him off to Pilate's residential court nearby. Here they accused Him of opposing payment of tax to Caesar (just days after He had taught otherwise) and of being an insurrectionary bent on overthrowing Caesar.

Pilate quickly saw through these sham charges. Profoundly impressed by Jesus' noble bearing and obvious innocence, he strongly desired to release Him. But hearing the mob's protest following his official exoneration of Jesus, Pilate groped for a compromise that would appease their wrath while sparing the life of this godlike Man. Under Jesus' scrutinizing gaze, Pilate felt himself filled with love and pity despite the fact that his life was steeped in crime and disgrace. How he wished to recuse himself from this case, but he felt he could not defy the mob.

It took more than knowledge of the law to stand for Jesus, more than a sense of His innocence, more than a sense of the treachery of His accusers. It took the power of His life within to turn sympathy and attraction into unwavering loyalty. That's what Pilate lacked. His love of earthly honor and position outweighed his attraction to Jesus.

Pilate then thought of an expedient. Jesus was a Galilean. He would send Him to Herod, the tetrarch over Galilee! This act of deference healed a long-standing breach between the two rulers, thus forging a corrupt peace through a common betrayal of honor. Herod, who had beheaded John the Baptist, was then in Jerusalem for the Passover. He had long wished to see Jesus, the miracle-worker. Rejoicing that Jesus was in his power, Herod personally interrogated Him before His accusers from the Sanhedrin.

But Jesus refused to answer Herod's questions or respond to his haughty demands for an exhibition of His healing powers. Jesus' accusers feared that He might display His supernatural abilities. But they need not have worried. Gladly would Jesus minister to the heartbroken and contrite who sought His blessing. But He would not satisfy the curiosity of those who would make a sideshow of His miracles while trampling on His truth.

Solemn indeed is it when God will not respond to the guilty soul dead in sin while yet living. Only to those entrenched in refusal to hear and obey, will the Living Word be silent. Enraged by Jesus' reproving silence, Herod ignited a carnival of violence toward the Prisoner. Jesus meekly bore the blows, mockery, and insults of Herod and his soldiers. In sarcastic repudiation of His kingship, they arrayed Him in a royal robe and made mock obeisance between their blows. But some in that riotous crowd, including Herod himself, came under conviction that the Man before them was God. Herod's rage spent and fears crowding in, he remanded Jesus back to Pilate without confirming the death sentence.

Once again the case was in Pilate's hands. He dreaded being the one to condemn Jesus. If only he could free Him at no risk to his own future! But having turned aside from the law of right, Pilate resorted to familiar expedients reeking with injustice. He declared that he would have Jesus scourged and then released. By this brutish act he hoped to appease the mob's enmity toward Jesus. Instead, he only fanned the flames of their rage. Jesus yearned for Pilate's salvation, so He made one final effort to touch his heart with truth. As Pilate wavered with indecision, a messenger pressed through the crowd with a letter from his wife, begging him to have nothing to do with that just Man, for she had suffered many things in a dream because of Him.

Pilate should have had *everything* to do with that just Man. He should have stood by Him as an ally, disciple, exonerator, and friend. But pragmatism overruled principle. At the last he would do the people's bidding. Having cast aside the shield of justice, Pilate became putty in the hands of the demonic rabble. He made writhing efforts to free the only Man he had found himself capable of admiring and almost revering. But love of power and position kept him from being valiant for the truth. So he declared, "Having examined Him, I find no fault in this Man. I have found no cause of death in Him. Behold your King!"

Noble words. Right and true words, all amounting to an acquittal—but spoken by one whose corrupted conscience would not be true to his judicial duty or convictions. In a final effort to awaken the mob's sympathy for Jesus, he brought forth the thorn-crowned Savior, scourged, bleeding, and clad in a worn purple robe, and proclaimed, "Behold, the Man." Jesus' innocence and nobility shone through the ravages inflicted on His countenance. Next to Him, Pilate placed the murderer Barabbas, on whose every feature criminality was stamped, though he bore no bruises. He intended that the people choose Jesus over Barabbas for release. When they wouldn't, Pilate called for a bowl of water to symbolically wash his hands from guilt. But his conscience would be stained till death. Jesus' affliction for our sins cannot be rinsed away with a ritual or waved off with a platitude. Our response to His claims constitutes our inscription over His cross. Is that inscription evasive, trite, and derogatory, or is it reverent, confessional, and lucid with recognition that only His sacrifice saves us from eternal ruin?

All that Jesus had suffered up to this point was but the prelude to His ultimate grief. May the Spirit strengthen us to march with Him to Calvary and there ponder His suffering love.

Throughout the agonizing ordeal of the betrayal, arrest, desertion, bogus trials, insults, and fiendish torture, Jesus remained calm and steadfast. He had no thoughts of vengeance. As He held in view the glorious outcome of His travail—the untold millions who would be redeemed by His sacrifice, which alone could save this graceless, guilty, demented world, Jesus kept steadily on course, rising above the avalanche of injustice that thundered around Him, above the shame of His mistreatment, above the yet greater anguish that awaited Him on Golgotha. Such towering love and courage, reverently considered, must surely conquer our hearts, win our eternal allegiance, and alienate us forever from sin.

"It would be well to spend a thoughtful hour each day reviewing the life of Christ. . . . We should take it point by point and let the imagination vividly grasp each scene, especially the closing ones of His earthly life. By thus contemplating His teachings and sufferings, and the infinite sacrifice made by Him for the redemption of the race, we may strengthen our faith, quicken our love, and become more deeply imbued with the spirit which sustained our Saviour. . . . Everything noble and generous in man will respond to the contemplation of Christ upon the cross."[5]

1. Ellen G. White, *The Desire of Ages* (Nampa, Idaho: Pacific Press®, 1940), 694.
2. Ibid., 700–703.
3. Ibid., 710.
4. Ibid., 712, 713.
5. Ellen G. White, *Testimonies for the Church* (Nampa, Idaho: Pacific Press®, 1948), 4:374.

O the Bleeding Lamb!

In his book *Fifty Years in the Church of Rome,* Charles Chiniquy, apostle of temperance, says that in childhood he often read passages of Scripture aloud to his mother and discussed their significance with her. He records that on one occasion, when he was nine, "While reading the history of the sufferings of the Saviour, my young heart was so much impressed that I could hardly enunciate the words, and my voice trembled. My mother, perceiving my emotion, tried to say something on the love of Jesus for us, but she could not utter a word; her voice was suffocated by her sobs. She leaned her head on my forehead, and I felt two streams of tears falling from her eyes on my cheeks. . . . I wept also; and my tears were mixed with hers. The holy book fell from my hands, and I threw myself into my dear mother's arms.

"No human words can express [what we felt] in that most blessed hour. No! I will never forget that solemn hour when my mother's heart was perfectly blended with mine at the feet of our dying Saviour. There was a real perfume from heaven in those my mother's tears which were flowing on me. It seemed that . . . there was a celestial harmony in the sound of her voice and in her sobs. Though more than half a century has passed since that solemn hour when Jesus, for the first time, revealed to me something of His suffering and His love, my heart leaps with joy every time I think of it."

May the Lord help us approach Calvary with the same reverential awe Chiniquy and his mother had as they read the Crucifixion story that memorable day in his childhood. One can best appreciate the record of the Crucifixion—indeed the whole account of the Passion Week—by reading the story in synoptic form, as told by Matthew, Mark, Luke, and John. By studying this fourfold parallax view of the action, we can catch every nuance of insight that the Holy Spirit saw fit to impress upon the minds and memories of the Gospel writers.

When contemplating Calvary, the stellar focus that illuminates every attendant circumstance is this: "Christ died for our sins according to the scriptures" (1 Corinthians 15:3). We cannot reduce His crucifixion to a mere martyrdom or egregious aberration of justice. Bible prophecy vividly foretells all the leading features of that fateful event, thus ruling out chance. Also, the spiritual dynamics and supernatural occurrences that attended the Crucifixion mark its unparalleled significance. Jesus' sufferings borne on Calvary are the means by which the gates of everlasting life are opened to us if only we accept His sacrifice on our behalf. Jesus willingly endured the Cross for love's sake; the affliction was not inescapable or thrust upon Him by surprise (see John 10:17, 18).

Before the water of self-exoneration was dry on Pilate's guilty hands, Jesus was pushed from the court of infamy toward the place of His execution (see Matthew 27:31, 32; Luke 23:26-33). History designates the route from Pilate's judgment hall to Calvary as the *Via Dolorosa,* "the way of pain (or anguish)." Short though the distance was, Jesus' passage over it was agonizingly slow. The weight of the cross rudely forced on His lacerated shoulders, the procession of soldiers overseeing the execution, and the turbulent, ever-increasing throng along the way impeded His progress. In His weakened condition, Jesus collapsed beneath the burden.

On Simon the Cyrenian, freshly arrived on the scene, devolved the honor of being drafted to carry the Savior's cross to Calvary. He "was ever after grateful for this providence. It led him to take upon himself the cross of Christ from choice, and ever cheerfully stand beneath its burden."[1] May we be willing to carry any cross God assigns, no matter how ungracious or humiliating its guise.

One sight along the way to Calvary especially attracted Jesus' attention. Luke alone records the poignant scene of women who, in contrast with the heartless curiosity of the gawking throng, wept in sympathy with Jesus for the treatment He suffered (see Luke 23:27-32). Though Jesus' grief had cosmic dimensions, He didn't reject their sympathy, so earthbound in scope. Looking beyond His own travail, He saw the impending doom of many who now pitied Him—doom soon to fall because of their unbelief in Him as the Messiah. Looking further still, Jesus saw the doom of the world that would scorn His salvation and recognize too late the voice and form of One who pled with their consciences during their days of opportunity under the green, sheltering tree of His grace (see Luke 23:29-31; Hosea 10:8; 14:8, 9; Revelation 6:14-17). During those hours of concentrated anguish, the whole weight of human ills was thrust upon Jesus. His life was the payment and antidote for the lethal debt He bore.

Jesus was taken outside Jerusalem to be crucified (see Hebrews 13:11, 12; Exodus 29:14). This was meant to betoken His criminality, but its heaven-ordained message is that His sacrifice as a banished Israelite invites all spiritual outcasts, Jew and Gentile, to come to Him for salvation. His rejection is our reconciliation.

Just before the soldiers crucified Him, they offered Him the customary relief of a pain-deadening drink, which Jesus refused on a vital principle (see Matthew 27:33, 34; Mark 15:22, 23). He had pledged Himself to bear our afflictions and would not cloud His senses or numb His nerves in order to escape any portion of our suffering and temptation, especially in His office as atoning sacrifice for the sins of the world. What a lesson this conveys for us to practice temperance in eating and drinking "that the fine nerves of the brain be not weakened, benumbed, or paralyzed, making it impossible for [us] to discern sacred things, and to value the atonement, the cleansing blood of Christ, as of priceless worth."[2]

To Bring Us to God

Short, bitter, and brutal is the sentence "and they crucified Him there." This mode of execution was designed to inflict mounting misery on the victim till the moment of death. As Jesus hung on the cross, rising waves of love for the lost race welled up in His heart, even through the insupportable pain and woe pressing upon Him. He died, the just for the unjust, that He might bring us to God. Even as Jesus' sufferings on Calvary are humanly immeasurable, so also are the results of this sacrifice of His that was inspired by a depth of love "which no sounding can ever fathom. . . .

"When our Redeemer consented to take the cup of suffering in order to save sinners, His capacity for suffering was the only limitation to His suffering. . . . By dying in our behalf, He gave an equivalent for our debt. Thus He removed from God all charge of lessening the guilt of sin. By virtue of My oneness with the Father, He says, My suffering and death enable Me to pay the penalty of sin. By My death . . . [divine] grace can act with unbounded efficiency."3

Jesus' enemies did everything possible to augment His shame and discredit His divine claims. His prayer that the Father forgive His executioners embraced the world, taking in every sinner who ever lived or should live, for we all share the guilt of crucifying God's Son. His sacrifice was for us all.

Jesus remained riveted to the cross not by spikes or malice triumphant, but by love unutterable, by grace that prevailed over the grim and ghastly dementia of evil. Consider the anguish of the Father and the angels as they observed the proceedings on Calvary. Only the knowledge of what Jesus was accomplishing for our salvation kept heaven from intervening to end this demonic orgy of injustice that was being flaunted before their eyes.

In God's overruling providence, He directed Pilate to write on a placard fastened to the top of the cross, "This is Jesus of Nazareth, king of the Jews." Jesus' enemies wanted the words to repudiate, not confirm, His status as king of the Jews. Thoroughly disgusted with their malice and his own cowardice, Pilate ordered that his words stand as written. It was God's will that it should be so, for truly Jesus is King of kings and Lord of lords.

As Jesus hung upon the cross, an almost constant chorus of ridicule ascended from most who had come to witness His execution (see Matthew 27:39-44; Mark 15:29-32; Luke 23:35-37). By their flippant blasphemies, the religious leaders intended to make the whole of Jesus' mission seem a cheap deception, a fatuous nullity that was ending in disgrace. Soldiers, priests, rulers, and people echoed one another's braying taunts and jeers. How readily evil leagues with evil to oppose good! And amid it all, the disciples' faith was paralyzed, crucified into rigor mortis on Calvary. Jesus heard not a word of encouragement or defense even from those most sympathetic to Him.

One ray of comfort did illuminate those hours of thickening agony for Jesus—the repentant thief's confession and plea for mercy (see Luke 23:39-43). His words epitomize the condition of us all. They take in the ruinous effects of human guilt, the glory of Jesus and His righteousness, and everyone's need of heartbroken repentance and clear faith in the one avenue of hope set before us. Jesus, by His words of pardon and promise to the dying thief, turned His cross into a throne of grace, a tower of triumph, a sure refuge for contrite sinners.

The repentant thief left behind no legacy of moral achievement. He leaned for his salvation solely on the merits of a crucified Savior. He could do nothing else to be saved, and neither can we (see Romans 5:5-11; Titus 3:5-7). Our acceptance with God is not based on moral endeavor, but on full submission to the atoning merits of Jesus' sacrifice. Had the thief survived, he would have made restitution for his crimes and lived in obedience to divine law, for such is the fruit of true conversion. And if he had gone back to a life of deception and crime, he would not have retained justification (see Ezekiel 18:21-24; Galatians 2:17[4]).

Shortly after Jesus' exchange with His companion in death, the most trying stage of His suffering on the cross began (see Matthew 27:45-49; Isaiah 53:4, 5; 2 Corinthians 5:21; 1 Peter 2:24). "It was not the dread of death that weighed upon Him. It was not the pain and ignominy of the cross that caused His inexpressible agony. Christ was the prince of sufferers; but His suffering was from a sense of the malignity of sin. . . . Christ saw how deep is the hold of sin upon the human heart, how few would be willing to break from its power. He knew that without help from God, humanity must perish, and He saw multitudes perishing within reach of abundant help.

"Upon Christ as our substitute and surety was laid the iniquity of us all. He was counted a transgressor, that He might redeem us from the condemnation of the law. The guilt of every descendant of Adam was pressing upon His heart. The wrath of God against sin, the terrible manifestation of His displeasure because of iniquity, filled the soul of His Son with consternation."[5]

On the cross Jesus drank a cup holding the distillate of the world's collective guilt and condemnation, from the dawn of humanity's rebellion to the bleak midnight of its consummation. This was no representative or partial sampling of sorrow. Jesus died in a state of actual abandonment by His Father. Without assuagement, He experienced in full the solitary grief of the second death that awaits every impenitent sinner. In a way that exceeds our comprehension, He who knew no sin truly became sin for us, that we might be made the righteousness of God in Him. He upon whom ultimate darkness descended for our redemption blotted out as a thick cloud our transgression. To scorn the sacrifice is to miss the transaction and remain an eternal stranger to its benefit.

If we see from such texts as Hebrews 2:9, 14, 15; 9:26-28; 1 Peter 3:18; and Psalm 85:10 the infinitely sublime exchange that took place on Calvary, the love of Jesus shall constrain us to dedicate our lives to Him with a fervor that needs no artificial stimulus. We shall never leave our first love, but experience a deepening and widening of it at every point of advance in the Christian life (see Ephesians 3:16-21).

"The cross of Christ is lifted up between heaven and earth. Here comes the Father and the whole train of holy angels; and as they approach that cross, the Father bows to the cross and the sacrifice is accepted. Then comes sinful man, with his burden of sin, to the cross, and he there looks up to Christ on the cross of Calvary, and he rolls his sins at the foot of the cross. Here mercy and truth have met together and righteousness and peace have kissed each other. And Christ says, 'I, if I be lifted up, will draw all men unto Me.' "[6]

Jesus' final words on the cross, "It is finished. Father, into Thy hands I commend My spirit," signify both the victory of His cause and His calm submission to the Father's keeping. Jesus emerged from dark despair to radiant victory. He died believing that His sacrifice was accepted.

Only the Way of the Cross

A procession of Old Testament prophecies foretell the Messiah's determination to die as a vicarious sacrifice for the sins of the world. This prophetic emphasis highlights the steadfastness and fully comprehending eye of God's love and the imperative necessity of Jesus' death for our redemption. Gethsemane proves that Jesus did not die because of a masochistic desire to experience pain and abandonment or some theatrical compulsion to display heroic magnanimity, but for the love of a sin-ruined world that He could not abandon to its otherwise hopeless fate. Jesus pled with His Father, with whom He is eternally one, for release from the horror of the Cross if there were some other way to save humankind. The Father's strengthening Him to endure that fathomless woe proved beyond all question that infinite love and wisdom could chart no other way than the way of the Cross. We would never taste the cup of salvation if Jesus had not drunk, uncomforted and alone, Calvary's cup of judicial condemnation.

Jesus' words "It is finished" signified not merely the termination of His human life but also the consummation of His sacrifice and the assurance of its success. Nothing could negate the completeness of the provision thus made. That which had so long been prophesied was now an accomplished fact of history. Henceforth His paramount task, and that of all heaven, would be to apply the saving merits of His sacrifice to the sin-stricken inhabitants of earth till the close of probationary time.

Those words, "It is finished; Father, into Thy hands I commend My spirit," uttered by the One who created all things by His word, resounded throughout the arches of the universe, guaranteeing forever the stability of its moral order and the joyous harmony of its fellowship.

The earthquake, lightning, and thunder that occurred when Jesus expired echo the majesty of events on Sinai and presage the triumph of His return. His law and grace operate as partners for the conquest of evil and vindication of God's rulership (cp. Matthew 27:51-56; Exodus 19:16-25; Revelation 11:19).

Jesus' death on the cross is the supreme manifestation of God's love, the supreme provision of His reconciling grace, and the supreme declaration that, while His righteousness makes no compromise with sin, it does make the ultimate sacrifice to give guilty sinners full opportunity to be saved and restored to favor with God. Jesus' blood shed on Calvary is the medium of every blessing we could possibly receive both now and in the future.

Read the graphic, moving account of Calvary's climax in *The Desire of Ages,* pages 756, 757. The rending of the temple veil betokened the accomplishment of Jesus' sacrifice, the opening of a new and living way into God's presence through His torn body, and the ending of the sacrificial system by divine decree as prophesied in Daniel 9:24-27.

Impressed by Jesus' sublime words and His noble endurance on the cross, the officiating centurion could not fail to recognize the divinity of the One who suffered there. He declared, "Truly, this was the Son of God!" This soldier's awestruck confession has been echoed down through the ages by people everywhere who have fixed their spiritual gaze on Christ crucified. And always in answer to this look of reverent faith, a cleansing fountain of mercy springs forth (see Zechariah 12:10; 13:1; 1 John 2:2).

Consider what the Father endured during the six hours of supernatural anguish Jesus spent on Calvary. He was agonizing for His Son, but by mutual consent not comforting Him, since Jesus' sacrifice had to be so complete that He died as a guilty sinner—or rather, as the composite of all sinners in every age—must die. It was not Jesus' divinity that died, for divinity is immortal. His humanity underwent the second death in our place that day. He served as a substitute for guilty humankind and paid our penalty in full. As the "Lamb slain from the foundation of the world" (Revelation 13:8), He encompassed the spiritual need of all humanity for all ages in the fullness of love that has counted the cost of our redemption and gladly paid it for the joy of the outcome.

Read the chapters "Calvary" and "It Is Finished" in *The Desire of Ages* (pages 741–764). Instead of skimming these chapters, immerse your heart in them, and absorb under the Spirit's blessing the rich revelations of God's love recorded there. No one can gaze upon Calvary reverently without coming away from the experience vitally changed. And none of those who so contemplate Calvary can ever really "come away from it." Rather, they will echo the hymn writer's vow, "I take, O cross, thy shadow for my abiding place; I ask no other sunshine than the sunshine of His face; content to let the world go by, to know no gain nor loss, my sinful self my only shame, my glory all the cross."

---

1. Ellen G. White, *The Desire of Ages* (Nampa, Idaho: Pacific Press®, 1940), 742.

2. Ellen G. White, *Testimonies for the Church* (Nampa, Idaho: Pacific Press®, 1948), 2:46.

3. Ellen G. White, *That I May Know Him* (Hagerstown, Md.: Review and Herald, 1964), 69.

4. See also Ellen G. White, *Christ's Object Lessons* (Hagerstown, Md.: Review and Herald, 1941), 314–318.

5. White, *The Desire of Ages*, 752, 753.

6. Ellen G. White, *The Ellen G. White 1888 Materials* (Silver Spring, Md.: The Ellen G. White Estate, 1987), 344.

He Is Risen!

R. W. Dale, a Congregational minister, sat at his desk one April morning struggling to gather thoughts for an Easter sermon to his flock. Though he was a learned theologian and accomplished writer, he could think of nothing worthwhile to say. Gloom darkened his mind. Intellectually he believed in God and the Bible, but at this moment his faith seemed paralyzed.

Unable to produce a thing, Dale walked to a nearby park. Braced by the fresh air, he observed new life awakening everywhere to the benediction of spring. As he heard the carefree children playing and saw swans rising majestically from the water on graceful wings, his depression began to lift as if wafted away by the breath of God. Then one thought flooded his mind, *Jesus is no longer entombed but is risen. He is risen, He is RISEN!* Never before had this stupendous fact so gripped his heart. He had always believed in Jesus' atoning death and resurrection, but now he began to *feel* the power of this truth as never before. Dale rushed back to his office and rapidly wrote out his message about the risen Savior, a message that enkindled new life in his congregation.

Jesus' resurrection validates the gospel and sets the seal to the truth of all Scripture. Through patriarchs and prophets God has traced down through the ages a golden thread of bright promise that the dead would live again by His power (see Job 14:12, 13; 19:23-27;

Psalm 17:15; Isaiah 26:19; Daniel 12:1, 2; Hosea 13:14, etc.). On the night before His crucifixion, Jesus declared, "Because I live, ye shall live also" (John 14:19). His impending ordeal did not signal the failure of His mission to give us eternal life; rather, it was the bond of its success. For "now is Christ risen from the dead, and become the firstfruits of them that slept. For since by man [Adam] came death, by man [Christ] came also the resurrection of the dead. For as in Adam all die, even so in Christ shall all be made alive" (1 Corinthians 15:20-22). Righteousness "shall be imputed [for us], if we believe on him that raised up Jesus our Lord from the dead; Who was delivered for our offences, and was raised again for our justification" (Romans 4:24, 25). We serve a *risen* Savior, not one whose history terminated on a cross.

On the day of Jesus' resurrection the disciples, with hopes crucified, huddled in the upper room, trembling for fear of being the next to share His fate. Then a mysterious stranger who appeared in their midst spoke with reassurance, "Peace be unto you." Only after He ate some of their food and invited them to touch Him would the disciples abandon their doubts and fears. Then in rapturous joy and wonder, they burst forth, "It is the Lord! He is risen! He is risen!" Their Redeemer had conquered sin and death! Now they knew that nothing could prevent the triumph of His kingdom. He had turned the cross from an emblem of crushing defeat into an instrument of glorious conquest. "Having spoiled principalities and powers, he made a shew of them openly, triumphing over them in it" (Colossians 2:15).

How the disciples rejoiced to be in Jesus' presence again, and how much more they prized His every word and look than they ever had before. Prior to this event they had been baffled and even offended by some of His teachings. Had they heeded His references to His approaching ordeal, they would have been braced for it despite the inevitable anguish they would have felt over the horrific events that attended His sacrifice. But now the disciples' faith was resurrected. They were prepared to listen to Jesus in a truly teachable spirit. And just as He had done for Cleopas and his companion on their sad journey to Emmaus, Jesus taught His eleven disciples from the Scripture all things concerning Himself. He introduced no new doctrines, but carefully restated the teachings that He had so methodically un-folded during His three-and-a-half-year sojourn with them. He de-sired their faith in Him to be rooted and grounded in Scripture and not in supernatural experience.

Jesus showed them from Scripture the redeeming purpose of His sacrifice. It was this understanding deeply imbedded in their hearts and minds that would make them an invincible force in proclaiming the gospel to the world. Under the Spirit's inspiration and in the fullness of their devotion to Jesus, the apostles would speak with pro-phetic authority in words that God Himself would immortalize as Scripture. That is why we can safely build our faith and Christian experience "upon the foundation of the apostles and prophets, Jesus Christ himself being the chief corner stone" (Ephesians 2:20). The foundation stones in the holy city, the New Jerusalem, are inscribed with the apostles' names, thus attesting that all who build on that foundation have chosen aright (see Hosea 14:9; Matthew 7:24, 25; John 17:20; 20:29-31; 1 Thessalonians 2:13).

God's Eternal Will

During His resurrection appearances to His disciples, Jesus did not change a single feature of His teachings. He had ratified His covenant in His blood and stated that His words would never pass away (see Matthew 24:35). Jesus the Living Word did not die on the cross so that He could change truths as eternal as Himself (see Psalms 89:34; 119:89, 152; 138:2; John 1:1-14). Moreover, a last will and testament is ratified by the death of the testator and is unchangeable after the testator's death (see Galatians 3:15; Hebrews 9:14-18). So all that Jesus taught and observed is to be transmitted faithfully, with-out alteration, throughout the ages. His gospel, righteousness, and law are coequally everlasting. They constitute His eternal will and testament (see Matthew 28:18-20, cp. 7:24-29; Luke 6:46).

Jesus bade His disciples tarry in Jerusalem until the Spirit be poured out on them from on high. They were to bear witness of Him in Jerusalem and Judea first and then in Samaria and beyond, to all the earth. His message of mercy was first to be extended to His mur-derers and all who had blindly followed them. Truly, the plan of salvation is tinctured with no bitterness or pretense of mercy; it is self-abnegating love through and through, reaching out to the roughest and most resistant of sinners.

On the night before Calvary, Jesus spelled out the Spirit's work on behalf of the church. He wanted to impress upon His disciples that the Spirit would be the indwelling divine Presence with them who would unite them in fellowship with Jesus and guide them into all truth, bringing to their remembrance Jesus' words so that they would never be at a loss to witness for Him. Additionally, the Spirit would impart to them every gift, grace, and idea needful for their development as Christians and their service for God. "The Spirit was to be given as a regenerating agent, and without this the sacrifice of Christ would have been of no avail. . . . It is the Spirit that makes effectual what has been wrought out by the world's Redeemer."[1]

In the days following Calvary, Jesus' disciples increasingly recognized their need of the Spirit. It is the mighty deeds for the advancement of God's kingdom enabled by the Spirit's presence and power that makes the book of Acts such a compelling record. God's Spirit came to give every willing recipient a new heart and a new nature fervently committed and fully empowered to do God's will. This transforming power kept early Christians unified in the truth and enabled the rapidly growing church to transcend the corrupting influences and customs that pollute every culture. The bestowal of the Holy Spirit was the secret of the early church's power, and it is the supreme gift of Jesus' sacrifice, for God's Spirit conveys all other gifts, graces, and capacities for glorifying God.

Jesus had no compulsion to brandish His victory in the face of His enemies. His purpose in appearing in Jerusalem after His resurrection was to present convincing evidence that His gospel is true. As He rose heavenward, Jesus repeated to the disciples the great gospel commission: "All power is given unto me in heaven and in earth. Go ye therefore, and teach all nations, baptizing them in the name of the Father, and of the Son, and of the Holy Ghost: teaching them to observe all things whatsoever I have commanded you: and, lo, I am with you alway, even unto the end of the world" (Matthew 28:18-

20). These parting words reinforce the central aim of Jesus' sacrifice—the reconciliation of the world to God through the regenerating power of the gospel.

As instructed, Jesus' apostles tarried in Jerusalem, awaiting the Spirit's descent. This was a time of humble heart-searching for them, a time to review all the riches of fellowship Jesus had offered them during His three-and-a-half years of discipleship training. How often they must have reproached themselves (not one another!) for the dimness of comprehension and dullness of heart that blunted their appreciation of the grace Jesus constantly poured out to them. They saw that if only they had been more receptive to His mind and motives, the spirit of rivalry and contention wouldn't have intruded among them. Nor would they have been annoyed by the actions and words of Jesus that so often disappointed their ambitions.

Now they saw that self should have been steadily on the decrease and Jesus constantly on the increase in their lives. But egotism had stunted their development and made His work for them much lonelier and more arduous than it need have been. Realizing all this, their love for Jesus and one another increased, and their hunger for the salvation of souls sharpened in proportion to the drying up of their thirst for recognition and honor.

Ten days after Jesus' ascension, "when the day of Pentecost was fully come, they were all with one accord in one place. And suddenly there came a sound from heaven as of a rushing mighty wind. . . . And they were all filled with the Holy Ghost" (Acts 2:1- 4). At Pentecost the apostles did not boast of their gifts or calling. Rather, they magnified Jesus, crucified and risen. They justified their every assertion with cogent applications of God's Word from Joel and the Psalms (see Acts 2:36-43). These features—a clear, correct use of God's Word and the glorification of Jesus' sacrifice combined with a direct call to repentance and to unreserved acceptance of the gospel—are the characteristics of genuine Holy Spirit revival wherever and whenever it occurs (see 1 John 5:5-12; 2 John 9; Revelation 1:9-13). As at Pentecost, Spirit-born revival produces the blessed fruit of strong, solid conversions, based on an enlightened response to the penetrating truths of Scripture (see Colossians 1:4-6; 1 Thessalonians 1:5-10).

Pentecost was not a one-time, climactic exhibition of spiritual power given simply to launch the apostles' mission. They continued to work in the spirit and power of Pentecost all through their remaining years of service. Though the power decreased during the subsequent years of apostasy, it is re-enkindled wherever hearts are fully surrendered to God. Soon the latter rain will fall upon the church, just as the former rain did at Pentecost—only the blessing will be much more abundant, enabling God's people to evangelize the whole world quickly with His final message (see Joel 2:23-32; James 5:7, 8; Revelation 18:1). This rich, earthward flow of heaven's power is a fruit of Jesus' intercession.

Our Merciful and Faithful Mediator

As the "Mediator of the new covenant," Jesus "appear[s] in the presence of God for us" (Hebrews 9:24). He isn't begging His Father to be merciful, for "the Father Himself loves" us (John 16:26-28, NKJV; 3:16). Indeed, the Father, the Son, and the Holy Spirit labor unitedly to save everyone and to produce full sanctification in every believing heart (Romans 8:26; James 5:7; John 15:1-7). Passages such as Hebrews 2:16-18; 4:14-16; and 5:9, 10, help us to understand that Jesus took our nature in order to be "a merciful and faithful high priest in things pertaining to God, to make reconciliation for the sins of the people" and strengthen us to withstand temptation by the same means He employed—prayer and God's Word applied through the power of His grace.

The prayer of Jesus recorded in John 17 epitomizes the scope of His high-priestly work. In this ministry Jesus retains His humanity as our Representative and Elder Brother (see 1 Timothy 2:5). "What shall we then say to these things? If God be for us, who can be against us? [That is, if we fully commit our lives to Him, who can interfere with the operation of His grace?] He that spared not his own Son, but delivered him up for us all, how shall he not with him also freely give us all things [needful for our redemption]? Who shall lay any thing to the charge of God's elect? [Satan will be your accuser, but God will refute all his charges and impute all of Jesus' righteousness to you if you look solely to Him as the source of all merit and renounce all self-justification.] It is God that justifieth. Who is he that condemneth? [When God justifies you, no one's condemnation of you will hold up in heaven's court, even though injustice may prevail against you on earth.] It is Christ that died, yea rather, that is risen again, who is even at the right hand of God, who also maketh intercession for us. [His intercession overbalances all our suffering and trials on earth and lifts us up into heavenly places with the Father and the Son at the throne of grace. Think of the privilege—and take hold of it!]" (Romans 8:31-34).

Jesus' sanctuary work does not diminish or supersede Calvary. Rather, it makes His cross a living power in our lives. It makes His crucifixion a fresh and vivid transaction that affirms the reality of our adoption. "Christ as high priest within the veil so immortalized Calvary that though He liveth unto God, He dies continually to sin [on our behalf], and thus if any man sin, he has an advocate with the Father."[2] We enter His heavenly sanctuary by faith in Jesus' atoning blood, which saves us and sanctifies hearts of believers (see Ephesians 2:13; Hebrews 10:19-22).

"The intercession of Christ in man's behalf in the sanctuary above is as essential to the plan of salvation as was His death upon the cross. By His death He began that work which after His resurrection He ascended to complete in heaven. We must by faith enter within the veil, 'whither the forerunner is for us entered' Hebrews 6:20. There the light from the cross of Calvary is reflected. There we may gain a clearer insight into the mysteries of redemption."[3]

In addition to His loving service as our Advocate and Intercessor, Jesus performs the final phase of His sanctuary ministry in the work of judgment (see Daniel 7:9-25; 8:13, 14; Revelation 4; 5). In this special work of disclosure, all who truly belong to Jesus are noted as exhibits of God's grace (see Hebrews 10:30; Malachi 3:1-6). Simultaneously, God invites the universe to judge His character. He presents a complete review of all the resources of infinite wisdom, love, and grace that He has exercised for the salvation of all (see Romans 3:4; Isaiah 5:3, 4). Satan is proven to be guilty of all the evil and failings for which he has blamed God. Jesus' eternal worthiness to rule the universe is established beyond question.

As the Lord presents us before the universe as His blood-bought sons and daughters, we do well to wait patiently for Him, imbibing His spirit of purity, grace, and loving service. Determined to repent of all sin, we must let nothing seduce or alienate us from believing in our Redeemer (see Psalm 37:1-7; Leviticus 16:29-31; 1 Peter 4:17-19). We must set our affection on things above and not on worldly pleasures and problems, which are all so soon to end.

At Pentecost, the people of Israel, pierced in conscience by Peter's tremendous gospel appeal, asked, "Men and brethren, what shall we do? Then Peter said unto them, Repent, and be baptized every one of you in the name of Jesus Christ for the remission of sins, and ye shall receive the gift of the Holy Ghost. For the promise is unto you, and to your children, and to all that are afar off, even as many as the Lord our God shall call. . . . Then they that gladly received his word were baptized. . . . And they continued stedfastly in the apostles' doctrine and fellowship. . . . And the Lord added to the church daily such as should be saved" (Acts 2:37-39, 41, 42, 47).

This passage helps us to understand that if truly converted, we are baptized into both Jesus *and* His body, the church—the two cannot be separated (see 1 Corinthians 12:13; Colossians 1:18-20). Further, we are to steadfastly adhere to the pure doctrines of Scripture and to the fellowship of the body, without which baptism quickly fades into a mere ritual without anymore significance than a play-acted wedding between two people who part soon thereafter.

With pens like probing tongues of fire, the apostles, in several major passages, set forth the true significance of baptism (see Romans 6:1-3; Colossians 2:10-13; 1 Peter 3:21, 22). Faith in Jesus' sacrifice, death to sin, burial of the old carnal nature, and rising to newness of life in Jesus constitute the fourfold significance of baptism. Our old nature is crucified with Jesus, and His grace now reigns in us through righteousness unto eternal life. This is a real transformation of nature, not just a liturgical notion couched in pious phraseology.

Jesus bade His disciples to "make disciples of all the nations, baptizing them in the name of the Father and of the Son and of the Holy Spirit, teaching them to observe all things that I have commanded you" (Matthew 28:19, 20, NKJV). "All who enter upon the new life should understand, prior to their baptism, that the Lord requires the undivided affections. . . . The practicing of the truth is essential. . . . The line of demarcation will be plain and distinct between those who love God and keep His commandments and those who love Him not and disregard His precepts."[4]

Jesus' Loving Gift

As a gift of love to those who have accepted Him as their Savior, Jesus instituted a special service on the night of His betrayal—the Lord's Supper. He established this ordinance to remind us of the unfading power of His sacrifice throughout the dispensation of His grace and of faith's ultimate reward—abundant entrance into the heavenly kingdom at His second coming (see Matthew 26:26-30; Luke 22:7-20). "As often as ye eat this bread, and drink this cup, ye do shew the Lord's death till he come" (1 Corinthians 11:26). In partaking of the Lord's Supper, we give a clear and communal expression of faith in these two gospel verities. As an act of appropriating and assimilating Jesus and His righteousness, the Communion service looks back to Calvary, the ground of our salvation, and forward to Jesus' second coming, the consummation of it. This service provides us with an opportunity to renew and extend our commitment to Jesus and to His body, the church, which He purchased with His own blood (see 1 Corinthians 11:27-32; 2 Corinthians 13:5). Foot washing is not an optional prelude to the Communion service, but an integral part of it (see John 13:1-15). Its observance by God's remnant church in these last days is one of the elements of the restored gospel as practiced in the apostolic era (see Daniel 8:11-14; Acts 3:19-21).

Four years after the *Titanic* went down, a young Scotsman rose at a gospel meeting in Hamilton, Canada, and said, "I am a survivor of the *Titanic*. When I was drifting alone on a spar that awful night, the tide brought the evangelist John Harper, also on a piece of wreck, near me. 'Man,' he said, 'are you saved?' 'No,' I replied, 'I am not.' Harper said, clear, full, and urgent, 'Believe on the Lord Jesus Christ, and thou shalt be saved.' Then the waves bore him away, but strange enough, brought him back a little later, and he asked, 'Are you saved now?' 'No,' I answered, 'I cannot honestly say that I am.' He distinctly repeated, 'Believe on the Lord Jesus Christ, and thou shalt be saved.' Shortly afterwards he went down; and there, alone in the night, with two miles of water under me, I believed. I am John Harper's last convert."

I do not believe that this Scotsman was John Harper's last convert, for someone reading these words today is going accept Jesus through the immortal testimony of that faithful witness for Jesus. If you've been floating on a dark, cold sea of doubt and fear, *believe on the Lord Jesus Christ, and thou shalt be saved.* He is not an impostor to be ignored nor a lifeless martyr to be revered, but a risen Lord by whom to be saved. He is a *risen Savior,* not an icon or a legend. He personally visits us all, seeking entrance into our lives.

Open your heart's door and say, "Lord, come in. Please save me from sin and give me a new heart, for Your glory and my everlasting good." He will accept your invitation—will you accept His?

---

1. Ellen G. White, *God's Amazing Grace* (Hagerstown, Md.: Review and Herald, 1973), 194.
2. Ellen G. White, *Selected Messages* (Hagerstown, Md.: Review and Herald, 1958), 1:343.
3. Ellen G. White, *Lift Him Up* (Hagerstown, Md.: Review and Herald, 1951), 329.
4. Ellen G. White, *Evangelism* (Hagerstown, Md.: Review and Herald, 1946), 308.

CHAPTER 10

Paul, the Champion of Justification by Faith

Much of Scripture's deepest theology of the Cross comes to us through Paul's teaching. His heart was set to draw every controversy and challenge to Calvary's summit—arraigning all, as it were, before the Cross. There mercy and justice were forged into perfect union through the fires of divine sacrifice. All of Paul's thoughts were held captive to Calvary; no circumstances or discussions could distract him from this unrivaled theme. "To Paul the cross was the one object of supreme interest."[1] Thus he declared to the Corinthians, "I determined not to know anything among you except Jesus Christ and Him crucified" (1 Corinthians 2:2, NJKV).

Paul's ardent insistence on the primacy of the Cross was not a cunning tactic to maintain a competitive edge over other theologians. The Cross was the wellspring of his entire life. His mind penetrated the living power of Calvary—or rather was penetrated by it (see Galatians 2:20). He conceived of Calvary as infinitely more than an historical event. He saw it as a living force, as the moral heartbeat of heaven's kingdom, the fountainhead of grace, the taproot of all spiritual power. For him the Cross was not an ultra-pietistic symbol offering escape from life's grim realities, nor was it an emotionally charged cloak behind which to conceal spiritual dearth and deformity. Rather, for Paul, the Cross was the living key to open the unsearchable riches of Christ. It was the glorious scepter that, for all who touch it, conveys forgiveness and the grace to live victoriously. It was the spring that irrigated his mind with inexhaustible gospel insight. It kept his labors fresh, fervent, and fruitful. He envisaged Calvary's redeeming purpose and was conquered, captured, and galvanized by it. For him to live was Christ, and this meant Christ crucified, resurrected, and interceding—and all preparatory to His reigning as King of kings and Lord of lords (see Philippians 1:21; 3:20, 21).

Paul's transcendent understanding of the gospel is not a tribute to his genius or accomplishments, but to the One who redeemed him and selected him for his work. Paul, church planter, preacher, and peerless pastor, was also an able expounder of doctrine and resolver of controversy. He effectively dealt with the broad range of religious debates that mark the entire history of the church, so racked by heresies, disputes, misbegotten notions, and tawdry sentiments that distort the gospel (see Galatians 1:6-8; 2 Corinthians 11:2-6).

Paul met this vast array of influences and ideas with more than scholarly intellect, more than diplomatic aplomb, more than prophetic insight, although he was in abundant possession of these faculties. For him the *aqua regia* of all controversy was the blood of Jesus, in all the fullness of what it represents. To Paul, the atonement was heaven's gold, and he would exchange it for no alternative or substitute. Thus any alloy, any base or spurious metal—no matter how cunning its composition or design, no matter how glittering its pretensions, how formidable its assertions—dissolves in the acid test of Paul's theology.

To Paul, whatever did not comport with Calvary was deception and dross. Recognizing how readily human "wisdom" lifts up its voice, only to darken divine counsel by false reasoning, he declared, "My speech and my preaching was not with enticing words of man's wisdom, but in demonstration of the Spirit and of power: that your faith should not stand in the wisdom of men, but in the power of God" (1 Corinthians 2:4, 5). For him, the purposes of God wrought out on Calvary were wisdom nonpareil, wisdom that shames and shatters every high thing that exalts itself against the knowledge of God (see 1 Corinthians 1:17-25). After all, what intellectual theory is going to regenerate the fallen nature of humanity; what ideology will redeem us from the moral ruin into which we have tumbled? Platonic thought, wrapped in its ethereal shadows, leaves human beings as naked and destitute as they were in Eden after eating the forbidden fruit.

Knowing this, Paul refused to let the smooth sophistries of scholars eclipse the Cross or shift it from its pivotal position in the scales of cosmic destiny. For him, the Cross was not an adornment or appendage to the plan of salvation but its archway and central pillar. "The preaching of the cross . . . unto us which are saved it is the power of God . . . and the wisdom of God" (1 Corinthians 1:18, 24). He knew that in the crucified One lodged "all the treasures of wisdom," knowledge, and love (Colossians 2:2, 3). For God to create a perfect order of beings calls for infinite power and wisdom, but for God to redeem and—without coercion—re-create beings rendered perverse and refractory through sin calls for the addition of infinite patience and love. Calvary is the means through which God accomplishes this transformation.

Knowing this, Paul made no allowance for priestcraft, ceremonialism, or specious spiritualizing to elbow their way between the Cross and its beneficiaries. Hence his inspired words of indignation to a whole region of believers whose faith had been subverted by ritualists who exalted Moses over Jesus and Calvary: "O foolish Galatians! Who has bewitched you that you should not obey the truth, before whose eyes Jesus Christ was clearly portrayed among you as crucified?" (Galatians 3:1, NKJV).

Paul's Encounter With Christ Crucified

When Paul met Jesus for the first time, he saw Him as the crucified Savior. Jesus personally revealed Himself to Paul in this striking manner (see Acts 9). This was fitting because until that moment, Paul was an entrenched enemy of the Cross. To him, Jesus was a legally executed impostor and His followers were renegades from Judaic wisdom, which he believed stood as this world's sole bulwark against heathenism and heresy. Paul thought he was doing God a service by persecuting Christians (see Acts 26:9, 10). He pursued his fierce hostility against Jesus and His church "ignorantly in unbelief" (1 Timothy 1:13; cp. Acts 8:1-5). His was not the ignorance of laziness but of a tenaciously held prejudice instilled through misguided religious education.

This perversion was the fruit of highly trained minds that sought to establish personal righteousness and acceptance with God by their zealous commitment to works of merit (see Romans 10:3). To them the assertion that human beings at their best are sinners and that the Cross is the sole means of redemption was an offense and stumbling block because of its unconditional negation of creature merit and its bringing all of humanity, Jew and Gentile, onto an equal plane of need (see Romans 9:30-33). From the days of its wilderness wandering, Israel conceived of its whole system of religion as one of righteousness by works. This misinterpretation of the gospel that God had revealed to them (see Hebrews 4:2; cp. Galatians 3:8) was not the result of faulty communication on God's part. He knew the sole means by which His covenant with Israel would be effective (see Exodus 24:8; Leviticus 17:11). But the carnal heart of human beings has an incessant tendency to mistranslate redemption's story into humanity's laudable response to God's requirements and the consequent earning of His favor.

Certainly, we are to obey God. But equally without question we are of ourselves powerless to obey Him (see Romans 1:5; 8:7). Only through the merits of a crucified and risen Savior can we receive the power to live in harmony with God's will as expressed in His Word. True obedience is the fruit of grace appropriated by faith. With princely passion and incandescent eloquence Paul pled with the Galatians to recognize this (see Galatians 3:1-5; 5:1-7). He didn't argue against obedience or depreciate its importance. He said far more about the necessity of obeying God than did all the other New Testament writers combined.* Yet we cannot miss Paul's militant opposition to the idea of obedience as the *root* of redemption. He insisted

---

* See any complete Bible concordance under the word "obey" (principally the Greek word *hupakouō* and its derivatives, e.g., Romans 6:12, 16, 17; 10:16; Philippians 2:12; also *peithō*, e.g., Galatians 5:7, cp. Romans 2:8).

rather that obedience is the indispensable *fruit* that bears evidence of genuine conversion.

Because Paul had been fully enmeshed in his nation's gross misconception of their own religion, after his conversion he was eminently qualified to expose the insidious web of fallacies that grew out of unenlightened "orthodoxy." No warrant existed for the legalistic interpretation of Moses and Israel's prophets that prevailed in the Judaism of Jesus' day (see John 5:39-47; cp. Luke 24:25-27, 44-47; 2 Corinthians 3:12-18; Galatians 3:8; Ephesians 2:19-22; Hebrews 4:1, 2). But the very misinterpretation against which Paul so ably argued has been taken by many modern Christians as the true import of the Hebrew Scriptures. Accordingly, some theologians regard the ideas of the Pharisees as representative Judaism, as Old Testament theology consummated. However, Pharisaism and true Judaism are diametrically opposed, as Jesus so often attested and as Paul so clearly expounded (see Matthew 15:1-14; 16:6-12; 23:1-39; John 5:40-47; Philippians 3:3). In utter repudiation of all that the sanctuary service and its richly instructive typology stood for, the Pharisees despised the Messiah's self-sacrificing love that inspired Him to pledge Himself to be the Lamb that would die at the cruel hands of those who pretended to be acting in His Father's name.

After Paul's conversion he saw that spiritual pride had prevented his understanding the Cross (see Philippians 3:3-8; Acts 26:9-15). Pride remains the chief obstacle to anyone's comprehension of the Cross. Paul also realized that Calvary's cross illuminates the entire Old Testament. Although trained in rhetoric, philosophy, and the sciences, he did not make them his reliance as the principal means of persuading people for Jesus. He chose instead the most despised but truly glorious feature of the gospel—the Cross. "I delivered unto you *first of all* that which I also received, how that Christ died for our sins according to the scriptures; and that he was buried, and that he rose again the third day according to the scriptures" (1 Corinthians 15:3, 4, emphasis supplied).

Human device would have said to St. Paul, "Make use of your philosophy as an introduction to your theology; call science to your aid; show the fitness of things; impress your audience with a respectful idea of your attainments in the wisdom of the schools; aim at the nerve of Demosthenes; put on the golden robes of Cicero; speak of your Master in his manhood, in his miracles, benevolence, and piety; compare his precepts with those of heathen sages; but cast a veil over his ignominious death, and the humiliating plan of salvation through faith in his suffering, till the public mind shall be somewhat inured to the less offensive features of his religion." "No," said St. Paul, "lest the cross of Christ should be made of none effect."[2]

Paul would not vitiate the power of Jesus' sacrifice or obscure its paramount importance by any cautious, apologetic approach to his subject. He saw that without the Cross, all religious discussion and performances were as barren as the offering of Cain. He advanced the Cross as the great weapon against sin and the great aegis for sinners to be rescued from sin's ruinous power. Paul combined doctrinal clarity with devotional fervor and effectual application. He presented the virtue that flows in healing rivers from Calvary—rivers that extend to the remotest bounds of earth and the least favored of lives. That is why his theology of the Cross has such a revolutionary effect on the mind of anyone who explores it fairly.

Paul's Understanding of Calvary

Paul's view of the Cross may be divided into ten interconnecting phases: revelation, propitiation, justification and pardon, reconciliation, regeneration, purification, empowering, identification, restoration, and unification. All these aspects coalesce in full completeness and are the sum of eternal glory. Generally we gain a richer sense of the whole by considering its various parts, much as we see a glorious array of colors when we view light through a prism. An accurate analysis of the parts enables us to appreciate the beauty and harmony of the synthesis. So, let's take a brief look at the glory of the Cross through the prism of Paul's mind.

1. Revelation. Paul saw streaming from the Cross God's mysterious, marvelous love, which is a principle of self-sacrificing commitment to the highest good of all. From the beginning, all Creation understood that God is love, and it flourished in the genial rays of this truth. But only when sin arose through Satan's defection did love's most sublime qualities manifest themselves—mercy, forgiveness, and self-abnegating service (see Romans 16:25, 26; Ephesians 3:8, 9).

2. Propitiation. Paul extols Jesus, "whom God set forth to be a propitiation by His blood, through faith, to demonstrate His righteousness, because in His forbearance God had passed over the sins that were previously committed" (Romans 3:25, NKJV). Paul conceived of "propitiation" * as atoning sacrifice, merciful substitution. This view of propitiation infinitely transcends the pagan concept of the term. Heathen cultures were well familiar with the idea of making expiatory sacrifices to appease the wrath or procure the favor of their gods. These sacrifices cost the gods nothing; the worshipers offered them as a kind of bribe. In contrast, God's propitiatory sacrifice consisted of His enduring in His own being the irrevocable penalty of the broken law and all the devastating results of humanity's rebellion against Him. "Christ our passover is sacrificed for us" (1 Corinthians 5:7; see also 2 Corinthians 5:21).

3. Justification and pardon. Paul saw the Cross as the inspiration to repentance and the living fountain of forgiveness for sinners. No greater proof of God's pardoning love could be demonstrated and no greater inducement to repent could be given than that of the substitutionary sacrifice of Christ (see Ephesians 1:6, 7; Romans 3:21-26; 5:6-8).

---

* Greek: *Hilastērion.* The Septuagint translation of Exodus 25:18 uses this Greek word for the "mercy seat." This word also appears in Hebrews 9:5. The biblical view of propitiation is unique in that the meritorious sacrifice and expiation are not made penitentially by the sinner but vicariously by a merciful God who suffered the penalty of our sins to offer complete pardon and restoration to all who will receive Him. Consequently, under its entry for *hilastērion,* Thayer's *Greek-English Lexicon of the New Testament* notes the monumental quality of Jesus' propitiation. Calvary's monumental character is exhibited not in marble or mosaic but in marvelously transformed lives that are imbued with its power.

4. Reconciliation. Through the Holy Spirit's influence, the Cross exerts reconciling power on the hearts of sinners alienated from the very life of God (see Romans 5:8-11). This reconciliation opens the way for us, formerly dead in sin, to be saved by His life and benefited by His intercession, for Jesus' shed blood gives us access to God's throne, where we are sustained in the Christian life (see Hebrews 10:19; 4:15, 16; cp. Ephesians 2:13).

5. Regeneration. Through the Cross applied, we experience the new birth and the power of Jesus' resurrection becomes operative in our lives (see 1 Corinthians 15:1-4). Paul consistently associated Jesus' crucifixion with His resurrection (see, e.g., 1 Corinthians 15:12-24). He saw in the Resurrection more than the hope of being raised from the grave at Jesus' second coming. He saw that believers are to walk in resurrection power even in this life. This power prevails in our lives when we die to the claims of our sinful nature and come alive to the righteousness of Christ (see Romans 6:4-6; Ephesians 1:18-20; Philippians 2:8-12). To Paul this thought was not a metaphysical abstraction, but a concrete reality.

6. Purification. It is this writer's belief that Paul wrote the book of Hebrews. In no other New Testament epistle is the cleansing virtue of Jesus' blood so fully developed and extolled (see Hebrews 9:14, 22-27; 10:10-12).

7. Empowering. Paul regarded the Cross as the empowering force that enables Christians to live the life of faith and harmony with the divine will (see Romans 6:6; Galatians 5:24; Hebrews 13:20, 21).

8. Identification with Jesus. The Crucifixion welded Paul to the cross of Jesus in unfathomably deep and rich fellowship with Jesus (see Galatians 2:20). Paul's fervent identification with Jesus as his Substitute and Surety operated as a spiritual gyroscope in his life, steadying him through all the tests and trials he endured.

9. Restoration. Paul's mind joyfully dwelt upon the sure prospect of eventual and complete restoration of eternal peace and perfection throughout the universe as the result of Jesus' atoning sacrifice (see 1 Corinthians 15:21-28; Romans 8:17-23).

10. Unification. Under the plenary inspiration of the Spirit, Paul advanced a "unified field theory" of the cosmos, the binding principle of which is God's self-sacrificing love as manifested in Jesus to engender and preserve moral perfection and relational harmony throughout the universe, that God may be all in all. This is how Paul states it: "It pleased the Father that in Him all the fullness should dwell, and by Him to reconcile all things to Himself, by Him, whether things on earth or things in heaven, having made peace through the blood of His cross" (Colossians 1:19, 20, NKJV; cp. Ephesians 1:7-12).

Paul adhered to his resolve to know nothing except Jesus Christ and Him crucified. He fulfilled this objective in a far deeper way than by simply making the Cross the sole object of his discussion—he let the spirit of Calvary permeate all his thoughts and feelings (see Ephesians 5:2). For him the Cross was not a fetish or a mere liturgical symbol; he assimilated and lived out its principles.

From this vantage ground Paul was able to grasp and, under divine inspiration, set forth the meaning of the Cross. His view of the Cross is epitomized in his testimony: "God forbid that I should glory except in the cross of our Lord Jesus Christ, by whom the world has been crucified to me, and I to the world" (Galatians 6:14, NKJV). Thus his life became a conduit of Calvary's redeeming power (see 2 Corinthians 4:6-12; 5:14, 15; 1 Thessalonians 2:5-13). This is what gives such enduring force to his writings. They breathe the atmosphere of the Cross and exhibit the ineffable, measureless glory of the crucified One "who was delivered for our offences, and was raised again for our justification" (Romans 4:25).

1. Ellen G. White, *The Acts of the Apostles* (Nampa, Idaho: Pacific Press®, 1911), 245.

2. Charles P. M'Ilvaine, *A Charge to the Clergy of Ohio on the Preaching of Christ Crucified* (Islington Green, England: J. H. Jackson, 1834), 14, 15.

CHAPTER

The Maligned Cross

Bible scholar John A. Clarke visited a map merchant to select geography supplies for schools in Africa. After perusing over three hundred maps from a variety of publishers, he noticed that the journeys of no monarch, traveler, philosopher, inventor, or millionaire had been charted for general circulation. Only one person had this distinction: the apostle Paul.

Wherever Paul went, two major events happened: the light of the gospel shone abundantly, and the darkness of Satan's kingdom was banished. It was this stream of undying light that immortalized his journeys. Paul did not select his itinerary; he traveled as an ambassador for his Lord—sometimes in chains, sometimes unfettered, but always as a valiant representative of the Cross and never with false pomp. Calvary's cross was his chart and compass, and he went whichever way it pointed. This experience captures the essence of the believer's cross.

Jesus said "to them all, If any man will come after me, let him deny himself, and take up his cross daily, and follow me" (Luke 9:23). Rightly understood, this means, "Let the principles and aims of My cross be the guiding and directing influence of your life. Let the constraint of My self-sacrificing love and the example of My purity and service inspire your actions."

Paul wrote of this experience from its depths: "I have been crucified with Christ, and it is no longer I that live, but Christ that lives in me. The life I am now living in the body I am living by faith in the Son of God who loved me and gave himself for me. I refuse to nullify the mercy of God." "Those who belong to Jesus the Christ have crucified the physical nature with its propensities and cravings. If we live by the Spirit, let us be guided by the Spirit" (Galatians 2:20, 21; 5:24, 25, Goodspeed). Paul's words point us to a new life on a higher plane that excludes everything incompatible with heaven and embraces everything conducive to a life of godliness. It is a liberated life, no longer shackled to the tyranny of the flesh.

Such a life is a mystery to the carnal mind. Unconverted people will resent the transformation they see in those whose hearts have become havens of grace. Unwilling to admit the possibility that God has eradicated the converts' sinful desires and given them a new nature, they will attribute every noticeable reform to the church's socially restrictive influence. So if the Christian turns down an invitation to go to the bar, the dance hall, or the movies, they will say with a patronizing smirk, "Oh, yes, I forgot. Your church won't allow you to do that. I suppose you have to go to prayer meeting tonight instead."

Such sarcastic comments reveal ignorance of the joys and boundless horizons of a true Christian experience, for in God's presence is fullness of joy; at His right hand are pleasures for evermore—pleasures in which alcohol, drugs, smut, and frivolous entertainment have no more part than the lighting of a cigarette does in creating a beautiful sunrise or the chanting of a bawdy lyric in making the wood thrush sing.

Only to those who are strangers to the Savior and the joy of being a new creation in Him does cross-bearing—sanctified living—seem like a dreary, penitential exercise or a sanctimonious effort to acquire creature-merit, to curry favor with God. Neither Jesus nor the apostles remotely suggested that the believer's cross conveys saving merit. That is the exclusive property and proceed of Jesus' cross. Yet both Jesus and the apostles assert that everyone truly imbued with the grace of Calvary will be a cross-bearer, progressively crucified to sin and to all efforts at self-redemption. In this process, egotism dies, Jesus and

His righteousness permeate the life, and worldly delights lose their bewitching power.

Thus believers become crucified to the world and the world to them. Their affections are set on heavenly realities rather than on earthly illusions. They have hope in Jesus alone—hope that is neither fickle nor frail, but full of encouragement, assurance, and bracing energy. Their appointed cross is the scepter by which Jesus rules their lives with royal grace and sanctifying discipline.

Self-crucifixion is not outwardly dramatic. An intensely private, interior work, its processes offer no material for stagecraft. It is the believer's voluntary mortification of every unchristlike trait and impulse. It is being courteous when others are rude, considerate when others are selfish, friendly when others are hostile, forgiving when others are condemnatory. It is laying the ax of God's Word and will to the roots of our own corruption. Not self-created, the believer's cross derives its existence, energy, and efficacy from Jesus' cross.

Man-Made Crosses

If the "cross" we are carrying is comprised of resentment and seething anger at the injustices, humiliations, and disappointments of life, we may be sure that it is a cross of our own manufacture. It has nothing to do with the cross that Jesus denotes as the insignia of true discipleship. The believer's cross is not galling or degrading; it vivifies and elevates. It is never carried under compulsion, nor is it casually appended to the life. It must be voluntarily and resolutely embraced with an understanding of its implications. After all, it is the cross on which *we are crucified.* "Those who are Christ's have crucified the flesh with its passions and desires" (Galatians 5:24, NKJV).

To some this may seem like a denial or diminution of Jesus' atoning work on our behalf, as though Jesus' cross and the believer's cross were in conflict. Therefore, self-crucifixion may seem a kind of affront to the gospel, an ascetic do-it-yourself form of spurious redemption, having no more relationship to the gospel than do self-flagellation or other works of penance. But we must not forget that Jesus, who is supremely qualified to understand the work of grace in His atonement and who knows the spuriousness of creature-merit, is the One who stipulated cross-bearing as an indispensable condition of discipleship (see Matthew 16:24-26). Jesus is prescribing not a discipline that conflicts with His grace but one that conduces to the free flow of His merits and mercy.

Cross-bearing is not a penance but a royal honor, a self-transcending victory march. "The love of Christ constrains us, because we judge thus: that if One died for all, then all died; and He died for all, that those who live should live no longer for themselves, but for Him who died for them and rose again. . . . Therefore, if anyone is in Christ, he is a new creation; old things have passed away; behold, all things have become new" (2 Corinthians 5:14, 15, 17, NKJV). No legalistic heraldry here, no clatter of counterfeit consecration, but an enlightened acceptance of Calvary that engages heart and mind.

However, the practical experience of self-crucifixion, while bracing, is not clothed with dreamy romanticism. The struggles involved are often intensely, even superhumanly, demanding. "There are toils and conflicts and self-denials for us all. Not one will escape them. We must tread the path where Jesus leads the way. It may be in tears, in trials, in bereavements, in sorrow for sins, or in seeking for the mastery over depraved desires, unbalanced characters, and unholy tempers. It requires earnest effort to present ourselves a living sacrifice, holy and acceptable to God. It takes the entire being. There is no chamber of the mind where Satan can hold sway and carry out his devices. Self must be crucified. Consecration, submission, and sacrifices must be made that will seem like taking the very lifeblood from the heart."[1]

When we accept without complaint the need for self-crucifixion, we find an inexpressibly deep comfort. For self-crucified believers, even while contending with inner corruption, are at peace with God. They war against their own fallen state in the unfailing power of the Spirit; thus the warfare is not futile or self-destructive. This is not humanity against itself, but saved sinners against the residue and relics of their own sinful natures. The applied remedy is the gospel, which is the power of God unto salvation to everyone who believes (see Romans 1:16).

As Christians, we all confront a spectrum of inner evils to which we must be crucified. We all need

- crucifixion to sensuality and lust (sloth, ease, and self-gratification),
- crucifixion to worldly pride,
- crucifixion to spiritual pride,
- crucifixion to love of approval and popular acceptance,
- crucifixion to fear, resentment, rivalry, and revenge,
- and crucifixion to self—the summary of all that's gone before.

We need to be crucified to all internal qualities and all outward influences that stand opposed to God. This is what it means to be crucified to the world and have the world crucified to us (see Galatians 6:14). It is the disenfranchising of our carnal nature and living to glorify God with our whole being—physical, mental, and spiritual. "Knowing this, that our old man [carnal nature] is crucified with him, that the body of sin might be destroyed, that henceforth we should not serve sin" (Romans 6:6).

This change does not paralyze personality, initiative, or interest in life. Only evil is mortified; we are set at liberty to obey the will of God from the heart. "I beseech you therefore, brethren, by the mercies of God, that ye present your bodies a living sacrifice, holy, acceptable unto God, which is your reasonable service. And be not conformed to this world: but be ye transformed by the renewing of your mind, that ye may prove [discern and do] what is that good, and acceptable, and perfect, will of God" (Romans 12:1, 2).

"The cross . . . is to be lifted and borne without a murmur or complaint. In the act of raising it, you will find out that it raises you. You will find it alive with mercy, compassion, and pitying love.

"Through bearing the cross your experience may be such that you can say, ' "I know that my Redeemer liveth," and because He lives, I shall live also.' What an assurance is this!"[2] We see then that the believer's cross is Jesus' appointed channel through which He causes His richest blessings to flow into our lives.

Self-Crucifixion

Self-crucifixion is not a pretentious act but the divestiture of all pretension, the sober, unself-pitying relinquishment of all illusions, all selfish dreams. It is the crystallization of the believer's resolve before God: "Not my will, but Thine, be done." It is prompted by the realistic recognition that "not by works of righteousness which we have done [or could ever do], but according to his mercy he saved us, by the washing of regeneration, and renewing of the Holy Ghost; which he shed on us abundantly through Jesus Christ our Saviour; that being justified by his grace, we should be made heirs according to the hope of eternal life" (Titus 3:5-7).

Thy wounds, not mine, O Christ
Can heal my bruised soul;
Thy stripes, not mine, contain
The balm that makes me whole.

Thy blood, not mine, O Christ,
Thy blood so freely spilt,
Can blanch my blackest stains
And purge away my guilt.

"Thy cross, not mine, O Christ,
Has borne the awful load
Of sins that none in heaven
Or earth could bear but God.

Thy death, not mine, O Christ,
Has paid the ransom due;
Ten thousand deaths like mine,
Would have been all too few.

To whom save Thee
Who can alone
For sin atone,
Lord, shall I flee![3]

Two crosses stand before us all: Jesus' and our own. Neither cross is effective without the other. No salvation springs from the believer's cross—but no salvation is found apart from it either, for that cross is synonymous with Jesus' yoke. That cross harnesses the believer to the will of God, a will that proves challengingly unlike our own—until, by patient continuance in the fellowship of well-doing with Him, we reach the point where in obeying Him we are simply "carrying out our own impulses."[4]

"The cross He requires us to bear will create strength in us more than it consumes, and remove our heaviest burdens to take the burden of Christ, which is light."[5] "Every one who takes upon him the yoke of Christ, with full determination to obey the word of God, will have a healthy, symmetrical experience. He will enjoy the blessings that come to him as a result of the hiding of his life with Christ in God."[6]

We must never forget that Jesus' yoke is easy and His burden is light (see Matthew 11:30). The cross He apportions us is not a yoke of bondage. It is not an instrument of torture or punishment but of ennobling service and training for advanced privileges and responsibilities. It is a cross that Satan begs us to shun so that our lives will be barren and unfruitful in God's service and our hearts will remain encased in selfishness while we cherish expectations that the cross of Jesus has secured to us a glorious destiny.

To shun fellowship with Jesus' sacrifice and sufferings is to remain unfamiliar with His joy, His truth, and His love. "There has been so little self-denial, so little suffering for Christ's sake, that the cross is almost entirely forgotten. We must be partakers with Christ of His sufferings if we would sit down in triumph with Him on His throne."[7]

"Those that have made a covenant with [God] by sacrifice" (Psalm 50:5) do not regard themselves as heroic or sacrificial. David Livingstone, who as a missionary to Africa braved perils and trials of every description, declared to someone who extolled him for his sacrificial service, "I never made a sacrifice. Of this we ought not to talk when we remember the great sacrifice which Christ made when He left His Father's throne on high to give Himself for us." Yet the sufferings that Livingstone bore for the advancement of the gospel and the eradication of the slave trade in Africa, most Christians would shun as unendurable.

Let the world call it bleak, morbid, and gaunt, but the cross of discipleship lifts the soul into the clear, shining atmosphere of heaven, where we see Jesus not as a pale face on a medieval fresco but as the One altogether lovely, the chiefest among ten thousand, the Lamb of God who takes away the sin of the world. The bars of that cross that seem so rigid to earth-bound vision are to the spiritual mind alive with invigorating grace. This cross turns the chilly atmosphere of self-care into warm trade winds of active compassion, aromatic with the opulent spice of godly love.

With Jesus at the heart's helm, the disciple's cross is the rudder in life's ship that keeps us from going adrift or missing our desired harbor. Such a heart knows the joys of sailing heavenward freely, having its decks covered with silver and its hull with yellow gold.

1. Ellen G. White, *That I May Know Him* (Hagerstown, Md.: Review and Herald, 1964), 280.

2. Ellen G. White, *Sons and Daughters of God* (Hagerstown, Md.: Review and Herald, 1983), 245.

3. From the poem "The Sinbearer," by Horatius Bonar, *Hymns of Faith and Hope,* First Series (New York: Robert Carter and Brothers, 1866), 150, 151.

4. Ellen G. White, *The Desire of Ages* (Nampa, Idaho: Pacific Press®, 1940), 668.

5. Ellen G. White, *This Day With God* (Hagerstown, Md.: Review and Herald, 1979), 212.

6. Ellen G. White, *In Heavenly Places* (Hagerstown, Md.: Review and Herald, 1967), 185.

7. Ellen G. White, *Testimonies for the Church* (Nampa, Idaho: Pacific Press®, 1948), 5:215.

CHAPTER 12

The Cross Triumphant

Calvary-love transforms our lives from a tense search for meaning to an energetic pilgrimage advancing on a sure path to heaven. Scripture reminds believers that they are spurred on by a "hope [that] maketh not ashamed," a "hope . . . both sure and steadfast, and which enters the Presence behind the veil" (Romans 5:5; Hebrews 6:19, NKJV). Yet, strangely, the power of Calvary remains little more than an esoteric metaphor to many who call themselves Christians. In consequence, their spiritual lives are tepid.

Such was the case with a gifted young minister of the Church of England, Henry Lyte. Scholar, poet, and diligent churchman, he discovered his spiritual bankruptcy one day when a fellow minister lay dying and called for Lyte to administer spiritual comfort to him. Then in his late twenties, Lyte was several years older than his ailing colleague. Feeling totally insufficient for this occasion, he had no idea of what to say when he came to his friend's bedside. To their alarm, both ministers discovered that they had no personal experience of the gospel; it was all academic theory to them. This was no time for liturgical platitudes, so they admitted to each other that they were strangers to God's saving grace, and they decided to study intensively together the plan of salvation.

As the two young men studied, their hearts were refreshed by salvation's story. Over the next several months, Jesus' cross became a luminous reality to both of them. Then the pallor of death fled from the young minister's face, and he forgot to die. Instead, he arose from his bed to spark a great revival in his district. And so did Henry Lyte, whose hymn "Jesus, I My Cross Have Taken" sprang from this experience.

When we permit the Holy Spirit to conduct us to the Cross, we experience a shattering change: Selfhood falls slain at the bleeding feet of Jesus. His goodness and willing sacrifice lead us to full and ever-deepening repentance for our sins. And vitalized by the inflow of God's pardoning love, we have a new life in Him. "One steadfast look to the Saviour uplifted upon the cross will do more to purify the mind and heart from every defilement than will all the scientific explanations by the ablest tongue."[1]

Through the revelation of God's character at the Cross, we will be filled with "the spirit of wisdom and revelation in the knowledge of him: The eyes of your understanding being enlightened; that ye may know what is the hope of his calling, and what the riches of the glory of his inheritance in the saints, and what is the exceeding greatness of his power to us-ward who believe, according to the working of his mighty power, which he wrought in Christ, when he raised him from the dead, and set him at his own right hand in the heavenly places . . . and hath raised us up together, . . . in heavenly places in Christ Jesus" (Ephesians 1:17-20; 2:6).

This is no artificial excitement, no hyperbolic form of mysticism, but the substantial reality and power of the gospel. In the believer's life, Jesus' grace is woven into every phase of character development, every action, every relationship.

But we are all so frail. All of us are familiar with the shame of failing to represent our Lord aright to others. We surrender to unchristlike feelings, to selfish, fretful thoughts and actions. Our main problem is not flawed genes or unfavorable conditions for the development of Christian character—it is blindness to the grand implications and power of the Cross. We need to be irrevocably crucified with Jesus; then we shall not waver. It is the cross of Jesus that places the human mind on the proper level, both now and in future glory.

God's redeemed people, standing on Mount Zion with the Lamb, are elevated to the highest eminence anyone could occupy. They don't place the Cross down in the valley of ancient history nor on a distant horizon draped with the mist of fading nostalgia. Rather, they realize that all that Calvary signifies stands immortalized in the Lamb, whose reconciling love shines forth through His servants in deeds of kindness and songs of praise. Followers of the Lamb do not see the Cross as an adjunct to Christian experience, but as its axis, its mainspring, its standard—its all-encompassing power. "Without the cross, man could have no union with the Father. On it depends our every hope. From it shines the light of the Saviour's love; and when at the foot of the cross the sinner looks up to the One who died to save him, he may rejoice with fulness of joy; for his sins are pardoned. Kneeling in faith at the cross, he has reached the highest place to which man can attain."[2]

True Character Development

The Cross annihilates all egotism while also promoting true character development. It enables those who are filled with its power to be transparent agencies through which God's attracting love can work. The singleness of mind that is a fruit of focusing on the Cross frees us to live for God's glory. Jesus declared that the one impelling force that would transcend time and culture, caste, and creed is the Cross. "I, if I be lifted up from the earth, will draw all men unto me," He said (John 12:32). Jesus spoke these words on His last day in the temple, in the presence of Greek proselytes who came to Him in search of true enlightenment. Their visit confirmed to Him that His sacrifice would not be in vain (see John 12:20-33). For the joy that was set before Him—the joy of delivering multitudes worldwide from the bondage of sin and reuniting them with Himself and the Father—He gained fresh courage to endure the cross, "despising the shame" (Hebrews 12:2). "All the ends of the world shall remember and turn unto the LORD" (Psalm 22:27).

But the Cross's attractive and bonding power extends far beyond this little sphere that we earthlings inhabit. It radiates throughout the universe, making the hearts of unfallen beings eternally doubt free and rebellion-proof by revealing to them the supernal riches of

God's mercy and truth, His righteousness and peace. "It pleased the Father that in him [Jesus] should all fulness dwell; and, having made peace through the blood of his cross, by him to reconcile all things unto himself; by him, I say, whether they be things in earth, or things in heaven" (Colossians 1:19, 20; see also Ephesians 1:7-10). Scripture displays the cross of Calvary not so much for its death-dealing aspect as for its life-imparting power. Jesus was "delivered for our offences, and was raised again for our justification" (Romans 4:25). "If, when we were enemies, we were reconciled to God by the death of his Son, much more, being reconciled, we shall be saved by his life" (Romans 5:10).

It is the glory of the Cross that animates angels in their mission of serving as ministers for the heirs of salvation. It is the invincible power of the Cross that has sustained God's earthly witnesses across the ages, enabling them to brave fire, dungeon, sword, and the bleak chill of human indifference and contempt. Icy hearts are mysteriously melted and vivified by the power of the Cross glowing in the lives of God's faithful witnesses. Truly, "the cross stands alone, a great center in the world. It does not find friends, but it makes them. It creates its own agencies. Christ proposes that men shall become laborers together with God. He makes human beings His instrumentalities for drawing all men unto Himself."[3]

Living exemplars of Calvary-love—love that is fearless, unfainting, and persevering: these are God's true witnesses who work in line with the power launched at Pentecost. Thomas Vincent (1634-1678) was such a witness—and with him several hundred fellow ministers who all were ejected from their pulpits under England's infamous 1662 Act of Uniformity that practically outlawed every Protestant body outside the Anglican Church. England's most consecrated clergymen were thus turned into fugitives, forced to work in secret for God and His people.

The king's soldiers constantly raided the independent Protestant meetings that were held despite the ban. Pastors and parishioners alike were imprisoned and deprived of their property. Some were deported as veritable slaves to English colonies. Meanwhile, alehouses—many but thinly disguised brothels—proliferated in town and country. London sank into the depths of immorality, sin triumphed over righteousness, and religion became the sport of the masses. A new breed of lewd comedies brought crowds to the theaters night by night, while nonconforming churches remained closed and state-approved churches were sparsely attended.

Then something dreadful happened. In the early summer of 1665 a plague broke out in London, gathering force over the next several months like a raging storm. Victims generally died within a day or two of contracting the dread disease. Thousands succumbed every week, and terror gripped the populace. Many state-appointed ministers fled to the safety of the countryside, forsaking London's pulpits. But the city's inhabitants, so recently impervious to spiritual concerns, now desperately flocked to the churches. In response to the general clamor for preachers, the nonconforming ministers stepped out of the shadows of banishment and obscurity. No one challenged their right to preach now.

Thomas Vincent, a thirty-one-year-old nonconforming minister who had been driven from his parish by the royal edict of 1662, was in London during the plague year. In his book *God's Terrible Voice in the City*, he vividly describes the calamity, giving particular emphasis to its spiritual effect on the people. Too modest to mention his own intensely active role in ministering to the victims of the plague and the seekers for solace, Vincent describes the work of his fellow pastors who came forward to care for the abandoned flocks.

He tells how they preached every day at all hours, taking turns without rivalry or sectarianism, because the churches were filled with frantic seekers virtually around the clock. The preaching of these ministers was plain and direct; they made no effort to turn every sermon into a work of rhetorical art. Their words flew as flaming arrows from God's bow to lodge in the core of human hearts. Full of conviction and Pentecostal power were their messages, which exalted the saving merits of Jesus' sacrifice and the efficacy of His gospel to heal the soul of the most fatal of all plagues—sin. Such preaching had rarely before been heard in London.

These ministers had no fear of proclaiming the whole counsel of God. Not a syllable of flattery or frivolity marred their messages, but the multitudes, ravenous for truth, came pouring into the churches. Decisions made for Jesus were so numerous that each day yielded a Pentecostal harvest. God was in it, working through consecrated men to reach conscience-stricken people. Clearly, Calvary-love was the driving force behind the dauntless labors of these ministers. Had Vincent and his fellow preachers not intimately known Jesus Christ and Him crucified, they would have fled with the nominal ministers to safer havens and left multitudes to sink into Christless graves.

Ideally, the shortness of time and the brevity of life should not be the primary motivation that brings us to Jesus; the infinite attractions of His character should be paramount. But God's love for us is too great to spurn our rushing to Him for deliverance even under the stimulus of selfish fear. If we allow Him, He will quickly transform our carnal fears into godly fear, which is "the beginning of wisdom" and "a fountain of life, to depart from the snares of death" (Proverbs 9:10; 14:27, see also 14:26; 19:23).

The Power of the New Covenant

This brings us to the heart and soul of the penetrating power of Jesus' sacrifice—the power of the new covenant. This is the richest fruit of the Cross, which is a tree of life to all who partake of its offering. One may master a thousand facts about the Cross, but its chief benefit for us, its central aim, is to save us from sin and bring in everlasting righteousness (see Daniel 9:24-26). At the Last Supper Jesus revealed to His disciples that the new testament (the new covenant) was sealed with His blood, the saving merits of which we are to internalize by faith (see Luke 22:19, 20).

In Hebrews 8:10-12 and 10:16, 17, Paul reminds us of the operative elements of the new covenant. In the surrounding verses he makes it clear that this covenant is the direct product of Jesus' sacrifice on our behalf and that our access to the provisions of this covenant is through confessing and appropriating that sacrifice. It is a magnificently integrated fabric of truth: Through the authority of His substitutionary sacrifice, Jesus not only credits to us the righteousness that we have totally lacked but now makes it possible for us to become, by faith, partakers of His righteousness—living repositories of His moral nature as defined in the Ten Commandments. In addition, we receive full pardon of all sin and constant, direct access to God through the Holy Spirit. Nothing is lacking to make our restored fellowship and union with God complete. "The very essence of the gospel is restoration."[4]

The Cross opens up to us the path of progressive victory over all sin. As we journey through life in companionship with Jesus, new thoughts, new motives, and new sensibilities are awakened. Thus we go on from faith to faith, from grace to grace, from strength to strength, from glory to glory. In Him, our hearts are united to revere His name in all aspects of life.

We learn to respect His every word joyfully and to seek grace that we may become enlightened regarding His whole counsel and attuned to every nuance of His will in the application of eternal truth. Before the Cross, Peter felt at liberty to rebuke Jesus for His supposedly misguided conceptions about certain crucial matters—such as the necessity of His being crucified and the instability of Peter's allegiance to Him. But after the Cross, Peter's view of his own judgment became very humble and his concept of God's Word correspondingly reverent and submissive. Never again did he feel at liberty to sit in critical judgment of anything God had spoken, whether through Jesus or through His apostles and prophets (see 1 Peter 1:22-25; 2:1-3; 2 Peter 1:16-21; 3:15-18; Galatians 2:11-17).

Like Peter, as blood-bought followers of the Lamb, we learn not to dismiss any of God's words as inessential. Instead of shrugging off those parts of His Word that are disagreeable to our natural inclinations, we will say, "Open Thou mine eyes that I might behold wondrous things out of Thy law. Whither Thou goest I will go, whither Thou lodgest, I will lodge. Thy words were found and I did eat them; and Thy word was unto me the joy and rejoicing of mine heart: for I am called by Thy name, O LORD God of hosts. As the apple tree among the trees of the wood, so is my beloved among the sons. I sat down under his shadow with great delight, and his fruit was sweet to my taste. He brought me to the banqueting house and His banner over me was love" (see Jeremiah 15:16; Psalm 81:13-16).

Children of the covenant will desire the loftiest reaches and the deepest sources the Lord sets before the people whose hearts run after Him in response to His drawing love (see Song of Solomon 1:4). They don't ask, "What is the minimum standard I must meet?" but, "How can I live so that Christ is magnified in my body whether by life or by death? How can I so live that all I do is pleasing to Him?" When we regard the whole counsel of God as for our good rather than for the restriction of our freedoms or the banishment of our pleasure, then we will know the joys of true discipleship and sweetness of covenant bonds with our God. We will experience in the depths of our being the power of the truth that makes us free—free in the unshadowed fellowship of a Lord with whom we are becoming more and more intimate (see Psalm 16:11; John 8:32-36).

As one of our new covenant privileges, we have direct access to God at all times. No one has to wait in line; no one has to file an application for a future appointment. Jesus' blood is the passport that compels devils to shrink back in fear and empowers loyal angels to conduct us safely into our Lord's presence day or night. "Having therefore, brethren, boldness to enter into the holiest by the blood of Jesus, by a new and living way, which he hath consecrated for us, through the veil, that is to say, his flesh; and having an high priest over the house of God; let us draw near with a true heart in full assurance of faith" (Hebrews 10:19-22).

Jesus wants us to prevail on His grace far more often and far more intensely than we do. We grieve Him by neglecting to pour out our hearts before Him. American author and philanthropist Julia Ward Howe, in an effort to secure justice for a deeply wronged man, wrote to a U.S. senator, detailing the case and pleading for his interposition. Knowing his reputation as a humanitarian, she expressed confidence that he would take effective action. She received this curt reply, "Dear Miss Howe, I am so much taken up with plans for the benefit of the race that I have no time for individuals." Amused and stung by this piece of hauteur, Julia pasted the senator's note in her scrapbook and jotted these words beneath: "When last heard from, our Master had not reached this altitude."

Julia, a careful student of Scripture, knew that the Savior ever lives to make intercession for us. He declares, "Whoever comes to

Me, I will in no wise cast out." As long as we don't try to enlist Him to cater to our sins and selfishness, He will be our Advocate to grant anything we ask according to His will, which is always interknit with His purpose to make us agents to benefit others. Never a minimalist or a grudging almoner, God wishes to do for us exceeding abundantly above all that we could ask or think. No challenge or perplexity is beyond His reach.

Peculiar Circumstances and Temptations

Evangelist Webb Peploe met with a woman who was deeply stirred by his gospel messages and wanted to learn more. She had heard of God's power to give victory over sin, but when Peploe asked if she had so laid hold of Jesus as to gain the actual victory, she answered with a sigh, "Mr. Peploe, I am a peculiar person. My circumstances and temptations are very, very peculiar, [so] I cannot really expect such overcoming power as you have described."

"Well," said Peploe, "let's report this deficiency to God in prayer."

"How do we do that?" asked the astonished woman.

"It's simple. Just repeat these words after me: 'O God, I thank Thee for all Thy promises of overcoming power in Christ; but my circumstances and temptations are so very, very peculiar that I find them too strong for Christ to help me. I am sorry that He is not stronger to meet my case, but my case is so very, very peculiar, that I cannot expect to find His help sufficient.' "

When the woman remained silent, Peploe asked, "Why do you not say this after me?"

"Why, that is rank blasphemy!" she answered.

"Just so," he replied. "But this is only your thoughts put into words, and why is it worse to *say* this to God than to *think* it of Him?"

He continued, "Now let's try another approach. 'O God, I thank Thee for all Thy promises in Christ of overcoming power, and that though I am a peculiar person, and my circumstances are very, very peculiar, and my temptations are very, very peculiar, Thy grace is very, very peculiar, and abundant to meet my very, very peculiar needs and very, very peculiar difficulties in a very, very peculiar degree.' "

The woman saw the truth, embraced it, and went away rejoicing in the Lord.[5]

Jesus' sacrifice for humanity was designed to produce no meager results, no partial or patchwork redemption, but the full reclamation of every soul who truly desires to be saved. Constant surrender to His sovereign love and will is the secret of victory and growth in grace; anything short of this produces frustration and failure. We need to come to Jesus and confess our unbelief, our rationalizations, and our futile striving to attain salvation by treating Him as a supplemental savior while relying primarily on our own willpower to accomplish the job. Our religious experience may be full of intensity and earnestness, but if its upkeep is a joyless chore, we need to make a fresh start with Jesus. Much of what we call "faith" is really high-stress self-dependence on which we have pasted the label of Christianity. Jesus understands how defective and deformed our experience is, how many lie spiritually crippled and impoverished at the Gate Beautiful outside His temple. He does not despise us, but stretches forth His hand and bids us arise and follow Him.

Jesus is fully touched with the feeling of our infirmities, but He is not the only One who cares. On the night prior to His crucifixion, Jesus assured His disciples that the Father Himself loved them and that they could take their petitions to Him directly in the name of the Son (see John 15:26, 27). Nothing is too great for Him to bear, for He holds up worlds, He rules over the affairs of the universe. "The relations between God and each soul are as distinct and full as though there were not another soul upon the earth to share His watchcare, not another soul for whom He gave His beloved Son."[6]

When we know Jesus in this intimate way, we can confidently and lovingly bring others to our Father's house, because it is our familiar home. We will regard whatever seeming sacrifices we must make in order to reach people's hearts with the saving power of the gospel as unworthy of mention in comparison to Jesus' infinite sacrifice for our redemption. Like Paul, we will be inspired to count all things loss in order that we may win Jesus and have the joy of winning others to Him. Towering before us will be the unconquerable power of His cross, beckoning us on from victory to victory. And the results will be sure. Calvary-love lived out in this world by Jesus' disciples will dispel the thick darkness that engulfs society (see Isaiah 60:1-3). If Jesus' cross is to us the scepter by which He rules our lives and governs our affections, then we will be the sharp sickles by which He will reap a harvest of souls for His kingdom.

"This is the highest science that we can learn,—the science of salvation. The cross of Calvary, rightly regarded, is true philosophy, pure and undefiled religion. It is eternal life to all who believe. By painstaking effort, line upon line, precept upon precept, here a little and there a little, it should be impressed upon the minds . . . that the cross of Christ is just as efficacious now as in Paul's day, and should be as perfectly understood by them as it was by the great apostle."[7] May we become students of the Cross, not so that we can formulate a new theory of Jesus' atonement, but so that we can be conduits through which His reconciling grace flows in bountiful streams to all the world.

William Tucker was an English artist. One cold night when sleet was knifing down from leaden clouds, he walked the streets of London in search of an arresting subject to inspire him for a new painting. On a dimly lit street corner Tucker saw a young mother dressed in thin, ragged clothing. She was clutching a child to her breast while looking helplessly about, as if wondering where to find food and shelter, where to find a spark of compassion. Tucker had found his subject.

Standing in a doorway, he made a quick sketch of the scene. Then he returned to his studio, where he became wholly absorbed in depicting the pathos of the young woman's forlorn look that trembled between hope and despair. While laboring to reproduce her expression, long-suppressed thoughts and feelings began to well up in Tucker's mind. Superimposed on the woman's face, he saw Jesus looking at Him and saying, "For you I became poor that through My poverty you might become rich in love and power to serve the suffering and outcast. I died that you might live and bring others to Me."

Tucker thought, *Why do I spend my strength in trying to portray human suffering when God has called me to minister to the suffering?* Laying aside his palette and brush, he studied to be a missionary, eventually going to Uganda, where he served as a valiant soldier of the Cross. When implanted in any receptive heart, the Cross will produce such purposeful self-abandonment in devotion to Jesus.

"Behold the Lamb of God!"
(Habakkuk 3:3, 4)

On many pleasant sights our eyes have played
O'er ranges bright and fertile valleys deep.
On forbidden scenes they have also strayed,
Beheld, too, tragedies that made them weep.
But our eyes see all through a veil darkly
Until illumed with the sight of the Lamb,
Not prancing in fields, but bleeding starkly
On a cross—Love's eternal Monogram.
Riveting glory beams brightly from its bars
Round which all revolves, and all life takes rise,
And sublimity springs from unsealed scars
That heal sin's deepest wounds and make them eyes
Washed and wakened at the Fountain of grace
Flowing from the Lamb's hands and feet and face.

1. Ellen G. White, *Manuscript Releases* (Silver Spring, Md.: E. G. White Estate, 1990), 4:121.

2. Ellen G. White, *Sons and Daughters of God* (Hagerstown, Md.: Review and Herald, 1983), 222.

3. Ellen G. White, *Seventh-day Adventist Bible Commentary,* Francis D. Nichol, ed. (Hagerstown, Md.: Review and Herald, 1980), 5:1138.

4. Ellen G. White, *The Desire of Ages* (Nampa, Idaho: Pacific Press®, 1940), 824.

5. Adapted from Arthur Pierson, *Seed Thoughts for Public Speakers* (New York: Funk and Wagnall, 1910), 202, 203.

6. Ellen G. White, *Steps to Christ* (Nampa, Idaho: Pacific Press®, 1956), 100.

7. White, *Sons and Daughters of God*, 231.

CHAPTER 13

The Light of the Lamb Forever

In a council with his generals one day, Napoleon thrust his pointer at the map before them and said, "Gentlemen, if it weren't for that red spot right there, Europe would be mine." That red spot was England, the one country that stood between him and absolute dominion over Europe. And if it weren't for the red spot called Calvary, Satan would be free to exert deadly dominion over this world. But onward speeds the day when his tottering empire shall fall with a thundering crash. Jesus' triumphant declaration on Calvary, "It is finished," opens the gates of victory for all who would enter heaven's life through the corridor of His wounds.

"Tetelesmai!"—"It is finished!" This word of triumph assures us that sin, an utterly repulsive and illegitimate force, will be blotted out of the universe. Calvary unmasks the heartless brutality of Satan's regime. It also reveals God's indomitable resolve to conquer sin and death even though it meant giving His Son to shoulder our sins and die our death. This wondrous exchange is love's greatest marvel. By means of death Jesus conquered death; by means of becoming our Sin Bearer, He became sin's Vanquisher while incurring no loss of royal honor in this exploit, weighted though it was with odium and anguish beyond measure.

Calvary's consummating cry, "It is finished," also guarantees that righteousness shall prevail, with every injustice rectified, every wrong remedied, and restoration complete. Across blood-soaked battlefields, from the grim recesses of death camps, over nations where the lash of despotism has dehumanized the masses, in homes where cruelty has crushed love, the cry has often rung out, "Where is God? Will divine justice ever intervene? Will evil face its day of judgment and eradication?" The answer always is, "God is here. He cares. In all our affliction He is afflicted. Justice will bear sway, and love will conquer, finally and fully."

However, before we can be delivered from the evil without, we must be delivered from all evil within. Jesus, the gospel incarnate, performs this work of deliverance. His truth received will make us free indeed and fit us for His kingdom. He will finish in us the glorious work He has begun, perfecting what concerns us (see Philippians 1:6; Psalm 138:8). With undeniable justice He will put an end to the kingdom of darkness so that it will rise no more (see Nahum 1:9; Ezekiel 21:25-27).

Meanwhile, we are to account the longsuffering of our God to be salvation (see 2 Peter 3:15; Luke 18:1-8). It is for humanity's benefit that Jesus delays His return. God is never disengaged or dilatory. His focus is sharp; His actions perfectly timed. Not an absentee landlord but an active sovereign, He encompasses the whole range of human history from end to end—and beyond, to the endless new beginning that awaits His redeemed. He rescues all who desire salvation from sin's brutal reign.

Many in our world are weary of wrong-doing. Disgusted by their own unrighteousness, they long for purity and peace but have no idea where to turn. All these the Lord is drawing to Himself with the bands of love. Others revel in violence. Anger has turned their hearts into a rumbling volcano ready to erupt. Still others are emotionally cold as ice, without hope or God in their lives. Amid all this confusion, false messiahs—both religious and political—arise from every quarter. They promise redemption while they themselves are the slaves of corruption and pride. Jesus foretold these conditions (see Matthew 24:6-12).

Divine grace alone keeps this degenerate and confused world from entirely destroying itself. Human misery and brutality are not chargeable to God—rather they reveal what would happen on a much larger scale if God were not present to rein in human madness as He skillfully and lovingly carries out the work of redemption.

"The Saviour longs to manifest His grace and stamp His character on the whole world. It is His purchased possession, and He desires to make men free, and pure, and holy. Though Satan works to hinder this purpose, yet through the blood shed for the world there are triumphs to be achieved that will bring glory to God and the Lamb. Christ will not be satisfied till the victory is complete, and 'He shall see of the travail of His soul.' "[1] At His return He shall reap in righteousness and take to heaven all in whose hearts the saving truth of the gospel has found welcome reception. These are the immortal harvest of Calvary.

Message to a Dying Civilization

God sends a message that produces this harvest before the end of time—the threefold message of Revelation 14:6-12. It is the everlasting gospel that Jesus has decreed shall be proclaimed in all the world for a witness to all nations before the end shall come. His love finds ways to present redemption's story above the din of a civilization in its death throes. Not all shall be saved, but God grants everyone abundant opportunity to receive His saving truth and grace. This is His supreme will, which nothing can thwart. Even the most active and complex array of forces Satan musters cannot intercept the revelation of God's truth and love to every human heart. God's will is not subject to countermand. Here His entreating voice to all humanity reaches the apex of its crescendo.

Revelation 14's triad of messages contains words of invitation and warning, wooing and woe, skillfully compounded for maximum effectiveness in a delusion-besotted world. These messages portray no compromise with evil, no presentation of truth at a discount to suit modern distaste for sound doctrine. God has designed them to be the universal antidote to every species of error, sin, and disorder that has invaded human experience since Adam's fall. Strong medicine which we dare not dilute, they present the truth as it is in Jesus—unapologetic and unambiguous.

Jesus and all heaven are determined that the gospel shall yield its full benefits to every willing recipient, while Satan strives to sabotage the gospel, preserving some elements intact but altering and removing other parts here and there. Thus he spawns not only doctrinal confusion but also discord in the Christian world (see Galatians 1:6-8). Nevertheless, God's threefold message is designed to bring us back to the complete revelation of all Bible truth, for nothing in the Scripture is irrelevant to the gospel. The God who has given us the gospel has also given us everything else in the Bible. He does not cumber His Word with irrelevancies. This is why Jesus said, "Man shall not live by bread alone, but by every word that proceedeth out of the mouth of God" (Matthew 4:4). No doctrinal truth lives unto itself as a separate entity. All truth is rooted and grounded in love, and God is love—a love that was demonstrated with matchless fullness on the cross.

God's last message to humanity is designed to call us back to the whole counsel of God, all irradiated with the saving light of Calvary. Beyond doubt, the Cross is the key to the treasury of the unsearchable riches of Christ (see Isaiah 22:22, 23, with all its powerful allusiveness). Blot the Cross out of Scripture or place it in a corner as an auxiliary article, and the Bible would lose its compelling power as salvation's story. It would fail to have the coherence that springs from a single integrating force of supreme value.

"The sacrifice of Christ as an atonement for sin is the great truth around which all other truths cluster. In order to be rightly understood and appreciated, every truth in the Word of God, from Genesis to Revelation, must be studied in the light which streams from the cross of Calvary, and in connection with the wondrous, central truth of the Saviour's atonement. Those who study the Redeemer's wonderful sacrifice grow in grace and knowledge."[2]

Accordingly, the message of the first angel to "fear God and give glory to Him, for the hour of His judgment is come, and worship Him that made heaven, and earth, and the sea, and the fountains of waters" calls us back to honoring God on His own terms and receiving the complete light of His Word—all of which projects the richness and fullness of His saving purposes concentrated in the sacrifice of His Son.

Instead of being an assurance-robbing, antigospel element, the proclamation of God's judgment emphasizes the certainty that every receptive person is benefited by God's saving grace. In His judgment, God vindicates His name, His people, and the full efficacy of the gospel, in which justice and mercy, law and grace, work together in flawless concert. None of these balancing qualities displace the other or become reversed in their function. At the same time, God's judgment exposes the hypocrisy and wickedness of those who have acted deceitfully or cruelly in His name (see Daniel 7:9-25). His judgment clarifies issues that Satan has sought to make hopelessly obscure and sets everything in order.

In this judgment God has no reason to be ashamed. The judgment offers all reasoning minds an impartial revelation, fully examined and corroborated, of the glory of the gospel in its achievements. In the pre-Advent judgment and the final judgment after Jesus' return, "every question of truth and error in the long-standing controversy will then have been made plain. In the judgment of the universe, God will stand clear of blame for the existence or continuance of evil. It will be demonstrated that the divine decrees are not accessory to sin. There was no defect in God's government, no cause for disaffection."[3]

A second angel, blending his voice with the first, proclaims the fall of "Babylon"—the apocalyptic name for false Christianity. This message condemns the counterfeit gospel and its supporting forces that enact a spurious Sabbath—a movement that epitomizes worship grounded in works of the flesh. Drunk with false concepts that unite church and state, Babylon turns the entire world scene into a tragicomedy of pseudo-worshipfulness and blazing persecution of all dissenters. Instead of ceasing from its own ideas and works, Babylon promotes doctrines of demons and theories of men. Its superstructure of aggressive delusion fortified with mighty miracles draws all unscriptural religions under its wing in the last days, making it "the habitation of devils, and the hold of every foul spirit, and a cage of every unclean and hateful bird" (Revelation 18:2, cp. Ezekiel 22:24-31). Hence the call to "come out of her, my people" (Revelation 18:4).

Satan has so infiltrated the church that he has not only succeeded in tainting Christianity with profoundly false beliefs, but he has also taught its leaders to make virtually no distinction between the sacred and profane. Further, he has induced the laity to regard their pastors as nearly supreme authorities concerning Bible doctrine. How deplorably this contrasts with Paul's declaration to the true-hearted believers in Ephesus: "[You] are built upon the foundation of the apostles and prophets, Jesus Christ himself being the chief corner stone; in whom all the building fitly framed together groweth unto an holy temple in the Lord: in whom ye also are builded together for an habitation of God through the Spirit" (Ephesians 2:20-22, cp. Acts 20:27-32).

A Thousand Martial Trumpets

God's final message of warning in Revelation 14:9-12, which is amplified in Revelation 18:1-5, sonorous as a thousand martial trumpets, strives to awaken humanity from its fatal bewitchment with error, its blithe unconcern for truth, its delirious and hollow hopes. Jesus died to redeem us from sin and its wages, which is death. He is not willing that any should perish but that all should come to repentance. This accounts for the intensity and stern, impassioned stress of the third angel's announcement. Its pungent content conveys the unspeakable horror of the second death, an ordeal that thus far, Jesus alone has experienced. He bore this on the cross as our Substitute so that we would never have to so much as sample the drops of His wrath unmixed with mercy, let alone imbibe it fully.

This message, representing Heaven's last urgent appeal of love, exalts the Lamb of God against a backdrop of flaming destruction, for He stands between us and it, ready to pardon our sins and take them away, and waving as it were a fiery sword of warning to turn us from our rush to ruin. He pleads with us, "Behold My Calvary-love. Don't suffer the agonies of the second death with its final separation from God, which I have already endured for you. I triumphed over sin and death so that My victory might be yours. For you I drank the cup of divine wrath. Now I present in its place the cup of salvation.

Drink and live" (see Romans 11:22, 33).

Calvary stands as proof that sin, allowed to run its course, is bent on destroying God and stands implacably opposed to His way of love, purity, and righteousness. Sin in its full development is calculatingly evil and cruel; it is not merely a minor inconvenience or a variant path to progress. Calvary offers redemption to sinners but no refuge or rationale for sin (see Galatians 2:17).

In reminding us of sin's severe penalty, God intends to make us ask, "What is sin that it should so provoke God's wrath?" The answer comes back from the Holy Word: "Sin is the transgression of the law" (1 John 3:4). This realization, impressed upon the conscience by the power of the Holy Spirit, will lead multitudes to recognize that the Decalogue, including the Sabbath, was not abrogated at Calvary but is still in full, eternal effect. They will see that the plan of salvation was not designed to liberate us from obedience to God's law but from disobedience to it, and that this plan does not save us by the law, but exclusively by divine grace applied to hearts made repentant and new by the goodness of God.

For the lost, God's final message is the anguished cry of unrequited love, the sustained crescendo of a yearning, reluctant farewell that echoes and amplifies Jesus' parting words to His beloved city, "O Jerusalem, Jerusalem, thou that killest the prophets, and stonest them which are sent unto thee, how often would I have gathered thy children together, even as a hen gathereth her chickens under her wings, and ye would not! Behold, your house is left unto you desolate" (Matthew 23:37, 38). It is the poignant, searching query, "Is it nothing to you, all ye that pass by? Behold, and see, if there be any sorrow like unto My sorrow, which is done unto Me, in the day that I bore divine wrath for you, that you might receive My redemption and rejoice in it."

In its clarion note of assurance, the final verse in the message rings with the celestial majesty of an anthem composed in heaven: "Here is the patience of the saints: here are they that keep the commandments of God, and the faith of Jesus" (Revelation 14:12). God's gospel prevails to bring forth this clear, uncompromising result in the hearts of His people. They will stand without fret or self-merit, but in the beauty of holiness, saturated with divine love and grace. Their lives demonstrate that through the cross of Calvary, God has provided every facility necessary to bring us into union with Himself and each other. We are complete in Him.

"Through the cross we learn that the heavenly Father loves us with a love that is infinite. Can we wonder that Paul exclaimed, 'God forbid that I should glory, save in the cross of our Lord Jesus Christ'? Galatians 6:14. It is our privilege also to glory in the cross, our privilege to give ourselves wholly to Him who gave Himself for us. Then, with the light that streams from Calvary shining in our faces, we may go forth to reveal this light to those in darkness."[4]

Like the apostles at Pentecost, those who receive God's message will be blessed with the final outpouring of the Holy Spirit that magnifies the truth and authority of God's Word in the rich context of Jesus' atoning sacrifice (see Hosea 6:1-3; 10:12; Zechariah 10:1; 12:9-14; 13:1; Acts 2). Thus multitudes will be brought into a saving relationship with Jesus in fulfillment of His promise, "I, if I be lifted up from the earth, will draw all men unto me."

Along with their proclamation of the gospel, God's people will do the works of compassion Jesus has commissioned them to perform in this sin-ravaged world. Multitudes will joyfully come out of Babylon to welcome Christ and His righteousness into their hearts and to join His faithful remnant openly (see Isaiah 48:20; Joel 2:23-32; Revelation 18:1-5). Those who deliver God's final message and walk in its light will proclaim it not with gloom, but joy, for the joy of the Lord is their strength, inspiring many to courageously break out of darkness and walk in the marvelous light of God's unpopular truth.

All who adhere to the true gospel will face persecution similar in spirit and intensity to what Jesus suffered on our behalf. But the Lamb will return in glory to bring a climactic halt to this attempted holocaust and to receive to Himself all who have been washed in His blood and sanctified by His truth. All the rebellious then living will perish from the brightness of His appearing (see Revelation 7:9-14; 2 Thessalonians 1:6-10; 2:8).

New Life for Humanity

Ultimately, the Cross is not the story of death, but of new life for humanity—eternally secure life for the universe, a life that overflows with peace, purity, love, and every attribute of our gracious God, who lives to bestow on His creation bountiful blessings without end. This life was purchased—we can hardly say it too often—at the cost of Jesus' voluntary death. He died not to eternalize death in flames of fury, but to conquer it and to "open the life gates that all may go in." Jesus has "abolished death, and hath brought life and immortality to light through the gospel" (2 Timothy 1:10).

What a glorious abolition! By virtue of Jesus' death and resurrection, the last enemy that shall be destroyed is death. If we cherish this thought, then our own death will not be a frightening prospect, and daily death to pride will be sweet and desirable. Jesus is alive forevermore, and He bears "the keys of hell and of death" (Revelation 1:18). He declares, "Because I live, ye shall live also"; "I am the resurrection, and the life" (John 14:19; 11:25). This is the invincible comfort and consolation of the gospel. Those who despise His love and truth forfeit this supernal blessing. But none need fail to receive a soul-saving love for the truth; the choice is ours entirely.

All the redeemed in heaven will keenly appreciate that they have gained their royal citizenship solely through the saving merits of Jesus' sacrifice. Never will this truth seem repetitious or obsolete, nor will gratitude to Jesus for His sacrifice decline. Never will the redeemed tire of declaring, "Unto him that loved us, and washed us from our sins in his own blood, and hath made us kings and priests unto God and his Father; to him be glory and dominion for ever and ever. Amen." "And every creature which is in heaven, and on the earth, and under the earth, and such as are in the sea, . . . heard I saying, Blessing, and honour, and glory, and power, be unto him that sitteth upon the throne, and unto the Lamb for ever and ever" (Revelation 1:5, 6; 5:13). Praise to the Lamb will permeate the universe in a polyphony of adoration whose fervor will never abate nor its splendor ever fade.

"The cross of Christ will be the science and the song of the redeemed through all eternity. In Christ glorified they will behold

Christ crucified. Never will it be forgotten that He whose power created and upheld the unnumbered worlds . . . humbled Himself to uplift fallen man; that He bore the guilt and shame of sin, and the hiding of His Father's face, till the woes of a lost world broke His heart and crushed out His life on Calvary's cross. That the Maker of all worlds, the Arbiter of all destinies, should lay aside His glory and humiliate Himself from love to man will ever excite the wonder and adoration of the universe. As the nations of the saved look upon their Redeemer and behold the eternal glory of the Father shining in His countenance; as they behold His throne, which is from everlasting to everlasting, and know that His kingdom is to have no end, they break forth in rapturous song: 'Worthy, worthy is the Lamb that was slain, and hath redeemed us to God by His own most precious blood!'

"The mystery of the cross explains all other mysteries. In the light that streams from Calvary the attributes of God which had filled us with fear and awe appear beautiful and attractive. Mercy, tenderness, and parental love are seen to blend with holiness, justice, and power. While we behold the majesty of His throne, high and lifted up, we see His character in its gracious manifestations, and comprehend, as never before, the significance of that endearing title, 'Our Father.'

"It will be seen that He who is infinite in wisdom could devise no plan for our salvation except the sacrifice of His Son. The compensation for this sacrifice is the joy of peopling the earth with ransomed beings, holy, happy, and immortal. The result of the Saviour's conflict with the powers of darkness is joy to the redeemed, redounding to the glory of God throughout eternity. And such is the value of the soul that the Father is satisfied with the price paid; and Christ Himself, beholding the fruits of His great sacrifice, is satisfied."[5]

Viewing Calvary, how can we doubt the love of God or the power of His salvation? It is our privilege to contemplate this matchless theme with revitalizing freshness every day. God has taken the cross, that emblem of cruelty, and turned it into a scepter of grace that extends to us immeasurable mercy and truth, effective power and exhaustless glory—for the Cross is the moral axis on which the universe rotates. "His glory covered the heavens, and the earth was full of his praise. And his brightness was as the light; he had horns coming out of his hand: and there was the hiding of his power" (Habakkuk 3:3, 4). Those bright beams add luster to every saint's crown; they illuminate the holy city, the New Jerusalem, with the unfailing light of Jesus' royal law and redeeming love (see Revelation 21:23, 24). "Blessing, and honour, and glory, and power, be unto him that sitteth upon the throne, and unto the Lamb for ever and ever" (Revelation 5:13).

In the cross of Christ I glory
Towering o'er the wrecks of time.
All the light of sacred story
Gathers round its head sublime.

Bane and blessing, pain and pleasure,
By the cross are sanctified;
Peace is there that knows no measure,
Joys that through all time abide.
—*John Bowring, 1825*

1. Ellen G. White, *The Desire of Ages* (Nampa, Idaho: Pacific Press®, 1940), 827, 828.
2. Ellen G. White, *Sons and Daughters of God* (Hagerstown, Md.: Review and Herald, 1983), 221.
3. White, *The Desire of Ages,* 58. See also Psalm 9:6-16; Revelation 15:3, 4.
4. Ellen G. White, *Acts of the Apostles* (Nampa, Idaho: Pacific Press®, 1911), 210.
5. Ellen G. White, *The Great Controversy* (Nampa, Idaho: Pacific Press®, 1950), 651, 652.

The Cross

Stript, stretched and strung
On two rough beams of wood,
Our Redeemer was flung
While around Him the rabble stood.
Jagged spikes chinked as they were cast to the ground
A soldier knelt before the Lord
Whom angels love to worship
And swung a hammer to pound
With blunt rhythm the iron that gored
And bit into those healing hands
Holding them in the bloody grip
Of death's dark bands.
Withering words of scorn
Were slung to punctuate
The chorus of blows that rang
Stark, strident and sharp
From Golgotha that April morn.
All Heaven with long sobs was torn.
Silent was every harp;
No angels sang.
Galaxies grieved at every glistening thorn,
And here—with curses coronate,
Saluted with taunts and jeers,
His trickling blood His sole attire—
Christ hung an object to abominate.
Maledictions like icy spears
Shot from lips that feast on fire
Fueled by spite and demonic ire.
Yet from this grim eminence rained
Golden torrents of His grace
And peerless love unfeigned
To cleanse the foulest of our unholy race
And make His cross a healing rod
And highway to the throne of God.

—Brian Jones